SPICE ODYSSEY

Paul Merrett was born on the spice island of Zanzibar amid a melting pot of cultural influences. During his career he has spent time working in many exotic corners of the world. Paul gained a Michelin star at the London restaurants l'Interlude and The Greenhouse. He now co-owns and cooks at The Victoria near Richmond, winning Best London Gastro Pub at the Great Pub Awards 2011. Paul has appeared regularly on TV. He has presented *The Best*, *Ever Wondered About Food,* and *Economy Gastronomy* for the BBC, as well as making regular appearances on *Market Kitchen* and *Saturday Kitchen*. He is co-author of *Economy Gastronomy* with Allegra McEvedy. Paul is an ambassador for Compassion in World Farming and Freedom Foods.

PAUL MERRETT

SPICE ODYSSEY

From asafoetida to wasabi,
recipes to really
excite & inspire

Photography Jan Baldwin   Illustrations Anita Mangan

KYLE BOOKS

This book is dedicated to my mum, Delphine Merrett—friend, culinary inspiration
and enthusiastic consumer of all things spicy! Thanks, Mum...

Published in 2014 by Kyle Books
www.kylebooks.com
general.enquiries@kylebooks.com

Distributed by National Book Network
4501 Forbes Blvd., Suite 200
Lanham, MD 20706
Phone: (800) 462 6420
Fax: (800) 338 4550
customercare@nbnbooks.com

First published in Great Britain in 2013 by Kyle Books,
an imprint of Kyle Cathie Ltd
ISBN: 978-1-909487-10-9
10 9 8 7 6 5 4 3 2 1

Text © 2013 Paul Merrett
Photography © 2013 Jan Baldwin
Endpapers photograph © Jan Baldwin/Narratives
Spine photograph © 2013 Bernard Zieja
Design © 2013 Kyle Books
Illustrations © 2013 Anita Mangan

Photography: Jan Baldwin
Illustrations: Anita Mangan
Design: Anita Mangan
Prop Styling: Lesley Dilcock
Food Styling: Annie Rigg
Project editor: Sophie Allen
Copyeditor: Emma Bastow
Editorial assistant: Tara O'Sullivan
Production: Nic Jones and David Hearn

Library of Congress Control Number: 2014935477
Color reproduction by Scanhouse
Printed and bound in China by C & C Offset
Printing Co. Ltd

Contents

Foreword by Cyrus Todiwala, chef proprietor of Café Spice Namasté

It is not often that chefs get the opportunity to write about another chef's book, and, then to top that, for it to be one on a subject they are every bit as passionate about, too.

That Paul Merrett shared my enthusiasm for spices came as a bit of a surprise to me, but it was enough, along with the honor of being asked, for me to blurt out the word, "Yes!" without hesitation. I have known Paul professionally, of course, for several years, but as I've got to know him more and learned more about him and the similarities in our careers, my respect for him has grown. I got to know him for who he is and to appreciate the passion that guides the work he does. Finally, I learned that the man was born in Zanzibar and naturally grew up amid spices and the best cloves in the world. This book exudes the word SPICE at every stage and it is a topic very dear to my heart. All my working life in Britain has gone toward raising the profile of spices. I was delighted to be asked to write this foreword.

Paul's writing is humorous, down to earth, and from the heart. Finding out about his childhood, amid the wonderful aromas and smells of a very developed kitchen, involving myriad cultures, shows how these early experiences leave an indelible mark on one's life going ahead. What sheer luck, and what strengths must have been developed at an early age.

A life of fun and excitement develops into a deep love for what one does, and Paul's recipes are totally descriptive of that. As I read the recipes, they reminded me of my own childhood, of noisy and strong-smelling bazaars, of a mother who, before her marriage, learned to cook very little, who was moved from her comfort zone into a large, bustling metropolis, where her own personal style emerged with the help and guidance of seasoned elders, as she developed into a confident cook whose tasty food lingers on for all those that tasted it long after she is gone. She left a legacy in the hands of her son.

Paul makes you want to try his recipes, to work with them, and to enhance your own creativity and skills. His honesty shines through here, and he tells things as they are. He encourages you to be the judge of your own palate, to use recipes as guidelines and, once accustomed, go forth and conquer with your own spirit, to mold and change the flavors that suit you best. Advice like this can only be given by a chef who has total confidence in what he is doing.

Reading this book, one gets the feeling of working alongside a great chef, challenging his own senses and recapping dreams of flavors from his childhood. Lucky indeed!

Enjoy, I say, explore, I say, enter with gay abandon, I say, and create your own magic.

Pots & pens—an introduction

When I was 16, I opened an envelope and was dutifully informed by the Surrey County Council Education Board that I had failed every exam put before me, and that my life would now spiral out of control as I stared into the face of poverty and vocational underachievement (it didn't say all of that—my parents added some of it). I was actually unconcerned by my dismal exam results. I was young, life was fun, and I was upbeat that everything would turn out all right in the end.

The very fact that this is being written as the introduction to a book, with my name on it, may suggest that I was right and that I didn't need those test results at all but, were it not for my mother, things could have turned out a whole lot worse.

I remember a very uncomfortable conversation when she outlined my job prospects. It wasn't a long conversation! We talked about what I *wanted* to do (play center-mid for Manchester United, be the next Paul Weller, er, that's it) and then we talked about what I probably *could* do. On the latter list was cooking.

I had always enjoyed eating. I was actually very good at it. I was adventurous and had a big appetite, which suggested that a culinary career of some description might be the answer. As luck would have it, Guildford Technical College had a reasonable catering department and the academic requirements for enrollment were zero—this was looking like my kind of career! As I climbed upon my Lambretta and zoomed off for my first day at college, I may have dreamed that I could make a living from cooking, but I would not have even dared imagine that I might top up this living by writing a cookbook. This is actually book number 2½ (I co-wrote the last one) and I sometimes wonder if medical attention has ever been required within a Guildford bookstore as Paul Merrett's former English teacher collapses, in the cookbook department, on seeing the name of such a disappointing student!

Writing a book is always daunting. I should be well used to the process, but I still find myself full of dread and self-doubt. In case you are unaware of how these things are done, I shall explain the process in easy-to-understand stages:

1. Forget the traumas involved with one's previous book.

2. Have an idea around which the new book will be based. It might be Mediterranean cooking, or perhaps family food on a budget, or even spicy food.

3. Visit several publishers and "hard sell" your idea, claiming that you have the authority and expertise to write said book while desperately hoping they don't ask for references and past sales figures.

4. Sign deal, boast to friends, and drink beer.

5. Usually the morning after stage 4, wake up and PANIC!

Panic because you suddenly realize that you have signed a contract stating that you will produce a 208-page book full of insightful expert advice (remember that "hard sell" moment?) and over 80 original, glamorous recipes to boot.

My biggest fear is that no one will buy the book. My first two books sold okay, so I really shouldn't worry, but I still tremble at the thought of the guy across the street proudly telling me that he'd purchased my first book for $2 in a thrift shop. That really dents an author's ego, you know. As a chef my ego is no less fragile. I have spent a career trying hard to earn accolades and decent reviews to prove my worth as a cook.

A book feels very much like a statement of intent, a self-explained vision of what I stand for as a chef, and in as much, this particular book is one, given the opportunity, I was always going to write. Spice has touched my life from very early on. I was born on the spice island of Zanzibar, which is about 30 miles off the coast of Tanzania, East Africa. The island has an incredibly rich

Pots & pens—an introduction

cultural heritage. On arrival from the mainland, one can't help but notice the mishmash of buildings and architecture, the exotic aroma of culturally diverse foods, and indeed the several different shades of people, all of whom make up what is modern-day Zanzibar. The reason for such diversity has its historical roots in the dark and shameful past of slavery. In the nineteenth century, 50,000 slaves a year passed through Zanzibar city, or Stone Town as it is more commonly known. Zanzibar was also a major port in terms of spices. Arabic and European traders were frequent visitors, and it was not long before they realized that the hot climate with regular rainfall was perfect for spice cultivation. Cumin, cinnamon, cardamom, and ginger were all grown successfully, but it was cloves that became Zanzibar's major export.

I was born into this cultural melting pot in 1967, a short while after Zanzibar achieved independence. My mother (a South African with 1960s wanderlust) learned to cook in Zanzibar, and much of what she learned had strong Indian and Persian roots. Even after we made the move back to the UK, she carried on cooking curries on a regular basis, and her love of spicy food has been a huge influence on my own cooking.

Having graduated from Guildford Technical College, I did what all young chefs should do—I went and worked for as many of the day's great chefs as possible. By doing so I was not only honing my skills, but I was also unknowingly (and inevitably) focusing very much on the culinary style of the day, and back in the 1980s and early 1990s that style was still very much dominated by a European, and particularly French, *haute cuisine* approach to food. Asian food was around, but not thought of in terms of "fine dining." It wasn't until I went to work for a

brilliant chef named Peter Kromberg that I started to see ingredients such as cilantro, ginger, and a range of spices, all familiar to me as a child, being used in modern high-end cuisine, as a result of his own travels as a chef.

When I finally became a head chef, I had one purpose in mind. I wanted to win a Michelin star, and I would gladly have given every penny I'd earned for the honor of seeing my name in the red book! As such I once again turned away from more exotic cuisine to pursue a tried-and-tested European formula to achieve my ambition. Once I had achieved the Michelin star I relaxed a little and started to think more about ingredients that I wanted to use, rather than those I thought I should use, and slowly spices started invading my menu, but still in a very low-key way. It took a stern lecture from the finest food journalist of a generation to make me consider my spicy talents more seriously.

One lunchtime the said food journalist, Matthew Fort, popped in to review the restaurant. The kitchen was put on red alert and I was a little concerned that he had ordered, alongside the very French-influenced duck terrine and braised breast of lamb, a dish that I had been playing around with, which had very Indian influences—a seared fillet of wild sea bass on top of sag aloo with an onion bhaji and tomato chile jam. Knowing that a dodgy review can break a chef's reputation, I was worried as I approached his table. He said very nice things about the duck terrine and the lamb, and then he looked me in the eye and said, "The sea bass, Paul, tell me about the sea bass." So I hesitantly told him what I've just told you, about Zanzibar and spice influence, and he replied, "Young man, it was the best dish of all. I suggest you ditch all the French stuff and concentrate on dishes like that."

If I'd had an ounce of commercial instinct, I would have resigned there and then and pursued his suggestion by opening one of the first restaurants cooking fine-dining Asian food. I didn't, and I've enviously watched many of my contemporaries do just that and do it brilliantly. However, from that day I have incorporated spice within my menus to a much greater effect, to the point where I felt I had a book burning within me. And you've got it in your hands right now!

Things are very different these days. My home city, London, is full of fabulous restaurants from every corner of the globe, fancy-pants expensive establishments as well as many great local ones. Things have changed at a similar pace for the home cook, too. As the world shrinks, spices are taking over. Thanks to the gallant, albeit shady, endeavors of bygone European explorers, spices have been available to the cook for many years. But whereas they were once prohibitively expensive, for the exclusive enjoyment of only society's most wealthy diners, they are now, with a few exceptions, relatively cheap.

Spices are everywhere. From natural remedies, scented candles, perfumes, mulled wine, breakfast cereal, and whacky cappuccinos, to the UK's favorite dish, according to recent polls, chicken tikka masala. I hope this book has something for every spicy cook. The beginner need be assured that not all spicy food, by any means, will be mouth-burning hot. Much of the finest spicing is also the most subtle.

This book is a collection of recipes that I enjoy cooking and eating. It dodges between countries and continents with no apology. There are many classic spicy dishes that aren't included and some quirky home-invented ones that are. My only aim is to provoke inspiration and exploration, because those two qualities are always apparent in all of the world's finest cooks.

Open letter to family & friends

Dear family and friends,

This book seemed the perfect opportunity to get something off my chest. Over the years, many of you have enjoyed foreign vacations. When we were younger, these tended to be in Europe—Spain, Greece, Turkey, etc.—and as you've all grown fat and wealthy, your holidays have gone more to more exotic places like India, Mexico, Thailand, and Vietnam.

Most of you return with small presents, often in exchange for feeding the cat or, as I live six tube stops from Heathrow Airport, for providing free parking. My wife always ends up with something (normally alcoholic) from duty-free, while I get the same thing from all of you—a small wicker basket filled with tiny plastic bags of spices. As you hand it over, you tell me about the amazing market and the 100-year-old gray-bearded salesman who explained that these were the finest spices in the world. They are not—frankly, they're terrible, and you've been conned.

If you want to buy me whole star anise, black cardamoms, or cinnamon sticks, go online and buy them from a specialist shop. I guarantee that the small bag of "top-grade" finely ground saffron is at best turmeric, and probably years old. I'm not being ungrateful, I love your cat and I'd feed it for free, but next summer can I have a decent bottle of gin?

Thank you.

A short note about the recipes

I seldom pick up a cookbook and use *every* ingredient or follow *every* instruction. Cookbook writers are sometimes so passionate about *their* way of doing something, they make it seem as if that's the *only* way of doing something. I'm sure I can be just as intimidating, so, to counteract this, here are just a few words of culinary diplomacy...

Nearly every one of the recipes in this book is available for change if you deem fit (that said, some of the desserts are a little more resistant to change). If I suggest using an ingredient that your best friend hates, there is no point in you cooking it for them, so feel free to choose an alternative ingredient in its place. Obviously I think the recipes work just as they are, but I'm eager for you to try them out, whatever the cost!

When it comes to spices, it's very difficult to be exact every time. Tastes vary from person to person, and to this end I have tested these recipes on the taste buds of others, not just on my own, so I hope things are about right. Salt is worth a mention. As a young chef I used lots of the stuff. Since having children and taking more of an interest in such matters, I've cut down dramatically. Moderate amounts of salt do appear in many of these recipes through necessity in terms of flavor. If you wish to omit it, that's fine by me. When I've used soy or fish sauce, I've tended to leave out additional salt.

Finally, measurements are paramount. Great cooks *do* measure things, rather than chucking around estimates with gay abandon. Buy some measuring spoons—you'll be shocked to see that what you thought was a pinch is in fact a teaspoon!

A word about your shopping list...
and an ethical lecture

Ultimately it is your decision on where and how you do your shopping, but I feel a lecture coming on, so here are a few words on food ethics.

MEAT & EGGS

Being an ambassador for the RSPCA's Freedom Food campaign and also Compassion in World Farming, I've spent a good deal of time talking about the animal welfare standards employed by producers supplying my industry and the wider consumer market. A good cook has respect for his or her ingredients, and I do think it's now fairly easy to find meats of all varieties that have been farmed to the highest standard. Years ago, if I had wanted a chicken raised with just a little care and compassion, I would have had to phone up some sandal-wearing hippy in a farm cottage. That's no longer the case.

If you are at all unsure, read the labels carefully, talk to your local butcher, or accost a supermarket manager. The internet is not only a great source of information (both organizations mentioned above give excellent up-to-the-minute information), but also allows us to buy meat directly from the farmer. Of course farming to such exacting standards costs money, and ultimately you and I, the consumer, pay the extra cost. My suggestion is to eat less meat and, when you do, eat the best meat available. When it comes to eggs, the compromise is zero. Pay the money for free-range, uncaged, barn hens' eggs.

FISH

My Dad is a marine biologist and I can remember him delivering stern and scary lectures at dinner time on the state of the oceans as far back as the 1970s. The situation remains critical for many species, and unfortunately some of them are our favorite types to eat, so a little experimentation with alternatives is required.

All of the fish used in this book have been listed on the various websites outlining sustainable fish at the time of writing; however, situations change continuously, so stay up to date with what can be eaten and what is best avoided. Much depends on geography. Species in abundance in one corner of the globe are not necessarily numerous in another, so stay informed.

FRUIT & VEGETABLES

I'm going to neatly duck all the arguments about organic versus nonorganic production and simply say that, when possible, buy local and seasonal. Obviously many of the ingredients in a book written around the subject of spice are exotic ones available only in warmer climates, so you may, at times, depending on your hemisphere, need to relax the "local" stance somewhat!

Right, that's it—no more lectures on what you can or can't do foodwise. It's cooking all the way from here on.

Stocking up

This book is very much intended for those of us who enjoy cooking at home. As such I have tried to avoid calling on (probably expensive) technical equipment that I take for granted in my professional life, but would not dream of buying for my home cooking. The same applies for ingredients. A professional chef has immediate access to just about any ingredient required with the minimum of fuss, whereas in general the home cook must rely on what's available in local shops. That said, it would be impossible to write a decent spicy cookbook without occasionally straying into the unknown, so I thought a few tips on purchasing and storage might encourage the wary novice to try the recipes.

I'm certainly not suggesting that anyone should rush out and buy every ingredient all at once—that would be putting way too much faith in a guy who has only written two previous cookbooks, and could easily have written a dud—but my endeavors have resulted in a tip or two, so it's worth passing them on.

First off is a quick inspection of your pantry. If yours is anything like mine, it probably contains the vacuum cleaner, a dustpan and brush, the kid's dirty sneakers, and a plastic bag full of other plastic bags, which you fully intend to reuse one day. Above all this stuff are three shelves, which house all the dry ingredients we use to cook, at home, for family and friends. Toward the front are all the items that get used and replaced on a regular basis—rice, pasta, baked beans, vegetable oil, etc.—and behind this are the jars and bags of stuff we buy once, cook with once, and keep forever. I bet if you were to take out all those used-only-once-then-forgotten things, you would find a rather large collection of spices.

Spices are indeed dry and long-lasting—you could put a jar of coriander seeds in a locked vault for a hundred years and, when opened, it would look exactly the same. However, the purpose of spice is not visual, it's aromatic. Spices age within the jar and, as they do, they diminish in flavor dramatically. It's worth pointing out here that whole spices last longer than the ground version of the same spice—more on this on page 15.

Buy small amounts of spice at a time, from a store that restocks regularly, thus ensuring you are always using the most pungent version. Make sure lids are always put back on properly and find a reason to go back to that spice and use it up while it's still on top form. A good, witty, imaginative spice cookbook is an absolute essential to achieving this end—this one, perhaps! As you work your way through your spice collection, keep the emptied jars handy, because your enthusiasm for spicy food will lead you to make up rubs and mixes of your own, which you can then store in these recycled jars—ingenious, thrifty, and environmentally friendly!

The recipes here also call for bottled sauces of various types to be dripped, added, and stirred in, and again many of these may be lurking in your pantry, as they are in mine. I have, in fact, such a vast array of exotic Asian bottled sauces in my pantry that I know I will never get around to using them all up. Last night I encouraged my less than charming children to taste some soy sauce that was two years out of date. This morning they were still alive and well at breakfast time, so I had some, too, and found it to taste exactly as I recall it tasting two years ago, thus leading me to suspect that ready-made bottled sauces have a much longer aromatic life than spices.

And so to shopping. The supermarket is the obvious place to start. Most of us live very close to a supermarket (my wife sometimes seems to live in the supermarket, and has certainly spent enough to buy a medium-sized one of her own), so upon deciding on a recipe to cook, I expect most people will walk along the spice aisle, hoping that what they require is available. My own local supermarket is quite good, but only quite. No asafetida, or whole mace, or brown mustard seeds, or fenugreek. The answer is the internet. There are lots of fabulous online spice stores run by enthusiastic types who have roamed the globe looking for the very best and most exotic spices. Most divide their spices by country or region, meaning you will be able to experiment with the same spice from different parts of the world. You will also find interesting spice mixtures such as baharat or laksa spice, which certainly aren't available in my supermarket. I'm not going to point you to any particular site, but there plenty and most are excellent. Try a search engine, but be carefully when typing in the words "hot, spicy and exotic"...

Local ethnic markets are great for sourcing spices. I live very close to Southall, an area of London with a large Asian community, where the shops are bursting with fabulous collections of dried spices and fresh ingredients, many of which I've never seen elsewhere. If you're off on vacation, it's well worth visiting the local food markets and seeing what's available. I could easily spend an entire two-week vacation at the Istanbul spice market! One tip, though: many of the markets sell their spices from wonderful carved wooden bowls without any indication as to what the brightly colored contents actually are. Ask for names and write them down, because if you don't, that very spice will end up hidden forever, at the back of your pantry, above the smelly sneakers and the recycled shopping bags!

Tools of the trade

First of all, don't worry, I'm not trying to sell you anything here. As yet there is no Paul Merrett Kitchen range. (I'm not averse to the idea—it's just that nobody's asked me yet. If you're a kitchen utensil manufacturer and your budget's medium-to-large, give my agent a call.) The following recipes make use of various utensils and equipment. Some you will already own, but there may be a few items that you'd like to add to your Christmas list.

MORTAR & PESTLE

This really is an essential piece of equipment for preparing the dishes in this book, or any spicy cookbook. The recipes often call for dried spices and fresh herbs to be ground and pounded before use. There are many types of mortar and pestle available, but avoid fancy-looking porcelain or glass ones because they are way too fragile, while attractively carved wooden ones are too lightweight. Instead go for a heavy-duty granite or marble version. The mortar is the bowl-shaped part, and it's important to get the right size. If the bowl is too small, you will not have room to work the ingredients, meaning you will need to grind in stages, which is a pain. On the other hand, if the mortar is too wide, you will always be chasing stray unpounded bits around the bowl. I think the optimum bowl size for a domestic kitchen is 4–5 inches.

Because you will be pounding and grinding a huge variety of ingredients, many of which will be highly flavored spices, it's a good idea to keep the mortar and pestle as clean as possible. An old trick that works very well is grinding raw rice, because it lifts off all traces of flavor from both the pestle and the mortar.

ELECTRONIC SCALES

Buy a set that goes down to at least 1 gram. Weighing spices is important and, because they are such pungent ingredients, a missed or extra gram here or there can make or break a dish.

DIGITAL TIMER

Essential. At the restaurant every section has a timer. Buy a magnetic one and stick it on the hood of the stove.

DIGITAL PROBE

My mother would say, "I'm not Heston Blumenthal, dear, I don't need a digital probe." No Mom, you're not, and that's why you *do* need one! They are very useful for working out if a slab of red meat is cooked to your liking. As a rough guide, meat cooked to an internal temperature of 125°F will be rare, 130°F will be medium-rare, 140°F will be medium, and 160°F+ will be dry and horrible, or well done, as some call it . Obviously poultry and the like should be cooked to the higher temperature to ensure safe eating.

FLAT GRILL PAN

This flat, cast-iron grill pan can be heated to a very high temperature for searing of fish, shellfish, and some meat. Sometimes the grill pan has two sides, one of which is ribbed (see Ridged Grill Pan, below).

RIDGED GRILL PAN

Similar to a flat grill pan is a ribbed cast-iron pan that will leave "bar marks" on whatever you're cooking. Good for creating the chargrilled look or for cooking marinated ingredients that could stick to a conventional pan.

MANDOLIN

If this is going on your Christmas list, it's important that the purchaser does not confuse it with the small guitar of the same name. The best (and happily the cheapest) mandolins are the plastic Japanese types, which come with various blades. Using a mandolin is fraught with danger—use the guard provided!

THERMOMETER

At various points in the book a little deep-frying occurs. You may own a fryer with a thermostat, but most of us just grab a pan and pour in a little vegetable oil. A thermometer will allow you to regulate the temperature. As a guide, successful frying will take place at 340–350°F.

MEASURING SPOONS

Very useful when working with spices. This book, and every other one on the subject, will direct you to use a teaspoon of this and a tablespoon of that. They're cheap and cheerful, so make sure you own a set.

Using whole spices

Generally speaking, I prefer to buy whole spices and grind them myself when required. Spices keep much better whole than powdered. That said, not all spices are easy to find in their raw state so it's better to buy small amounts of spice powders regularly than large amounts in one go. For once, bulk purchase does not save money!

I know a little bit about wine and even less about perfume, but experts in both fields talk about "notes" when discussing flavor and aromas. Spices, widely used in scents and perfumes, of course, can also be discussed in this way. Many whole spices have intricate layers of flavor or aroma rather than just one consistent "note." The trick for the cook is to release as many of these as possible. Grinding a whole spice has this effect immediately. The finer the spice is ground, the more the aroma is exposed and therefore released. This is particularly important when preparing a fast-cooking dish.

Heat also releases a spice's aromas. At a chemical level these aromas are termed "volatile," which to you and me (cutting out a whole load of probably very necessary science!) means that as they are heated the aromas evaporate and leap out of the spice, allowing us to detect them. This is why most spices are added early on in the cooking process. The very best time to introduce the spice is when you are cooking onions and garlic at a high heat in oil. It's also the reason behind dry-frying the spices. First, let's just clarify that term. When one dry-fries a spice, no oil is added to the pan. The spice, or mixture of spices, is cooked in the hot pan alone, allowing these volatile oils to do their thing. The slight coloration, or "toasting," of the spice adds another dimension again. The spice is generally, though not always, cooled and then ground to a powder before being used.

I think the simplest demonstration of the pungency of a whole spice versus a powdered version of the same origin is to take two small spoons of vanilla ice cream. Sprinkle preground nutmeg onto one, and on the other finely grate a similar amount of whole nutmeg. The results speak for themselves.

The dishes within this section are all fairly quick and simple to prepare. With my restaurant-chef head on, I would call them all appetizers, but that feels way too restrictive. Many of them would make a fantastic lunch, a light supper, or even a mid-afternoon snack, so please don't feel that you can only make them if you have two more courses to serve afterward! In fact, most of the Asian-style food I have eaten has been a succession of smaller dishes with no beginning, middle, or end to speak of, and I think that's definitely the most exhilarating way of serving and eating food.

Appetizers, snacks & carefree grazing

While churning 2 quarts of sheep milk into a lump of Pecorino is beyond the skill (and frankly patience) of most of us, you can now add 'cheesemaker' to your family crest with this most basic of cheese preparations. Labneh is a popular dish all over the Eastern Mediterranean and throughout the Middle East.

Labneh is made by simply hanging Greek yogurt in a cheesecloth bag to filter out the whey. It's often served just on its own with pita bread, but I like to add a little spicy sumac and a bit of sweet fruit. Sumac is a flowering plant common in Africa. The berries of the plant are ground to a powder and used as a spice—they are very slightly citrus-flavored, with a great crimson color, perfect to sprinkle over the pure white labneh. 99

Homemade labneh with sumac, pomegranate & basil

SERVES 8 AS AN APPETIZER OR AS PART OF A LUNCH SPREAD

2 cups Greek yogurt

¼ teaspoon salt

1 teaspoon sumac

1 pomegranate

a few small basil leaves

1 tablespoon extra-virgin olive oil

warm pita bread, to serve

You will also need a large square of clean cheesecloth.

Line a deep bowl with a piece of clean cheesecloth. In a separate bowl, stir the yogurt and salt together. Pour the salted yogurt into the cheesecloth and tie the excess cheesecloth with string so that the yogurt is contained within it. Hang the cheesecloth bag over a bowl—if your fridge has wire racks rather than glass shelves, this should be easy; however, if, like me, you didn't consider labneh production when buying your fridge, I suggest you tie the cheesecloth bag to a wooden spoon and balance the spoon over a bowl (nifty, eh?).

Leave to drain for at least 24 hours (I occasionally give it a little squeeze of encouragement) or until much of the liquid has drained out and the remaining yogurt in the cheesecloth is thick and fairly dry but still creamy.

It's worth noting that people are not given their own plate of labneh—they barge, stretch, and jostle to get their share. Spoon the labneh into the center of a serving plate and use the back of a spoon to spread it out into a circle. Sprinkle a generous line of sumac right across the plate.

Cut the pomegranate in half and remove the seeds, then scatter these randomly over the labneh. Dot about the basil leaves, drizzle on the olive oil, and serve with warm pita bread.

66 The wonderful thing about the internet is the lightning speed at which the ignorant can be transformed into the informed. Three minutes ago I knew that the betel leaf was a green leaf from some sort of creeping, vine-like plant found in Asia. Four clicks later and I'm a betel leaf expert of some standing, and feel confident enough to inform you that betel leaf is often chewed and consumed for its mildly psycho-stimulating hallucinogenic properties, it's mentioned in the *Kama Sutra*, it can stain one's teeth horribly if chewed extensively, and… hang on, should this ingredient be in my book? Anyway, you should be able to find betel leaves in your nearest Asian supermarket.

I recently spent time cooking on a beautiful Thai island where betel leaf was served as a kind of snack before a meal. It was really fun assembling the little leafy parcels, making them as sweet, fiery-hot, or citrusy-sharp as desired. My teeth did not get stained at all, my libido remained unaffected, and I didn't suddenly feel the urge to pen a rock opera, so I figured this recipe was okay to send to the publisher. The dish is a sort of help-yourself appetizer, with everyone making the betel leaf wraps at the table, so your job is more about assembling the ingredients and less about spending ages in the kitchen. 99

Betel leaf wraps with ginger, crispy shallots, chile & broken cashew nuts

SERVES 4 AS A SMALL PRE-MEAL SNACK

⅓ cup peeled and finely diced fresh ginger

2 red bird's eye chiles, finely sliced into rings

3 tablespoons Crispy Shallots (see page 186)

2 tablespoons unsalted cashew nuts, broken up a little

1 lime, finely diced, skin and all

3 tablespoons finely chopped fresh coconut

8 betel leaves

FOR THE SAUCE

1 small red onion, finely diced

⅓ cup peeled and finely diced fresh ginger

4 tablespoons palm sugar

juice of 1 lime

4 teaspoons fish sauce

1 tablespoon soy sauce

From the ingredients list there is only item that needs cooking—the sauce.

Put all of the ingredients for the sauce into a pan and bring to a simmer. Cook until reduced by half the original volume—the warm consistency of the sauce will resemble sweet chile sauce (as it cools it may jam up a little more, which is fine). Chill until you are ready to serve.

Pile the remaining ingredients onto a large tray or cutting board, and serve with the sauce.

Now, your friends may be well-traveled, worldly-wise types, in which case you can rely on them knowing what to do with this array of odd ingredients. However, just in case they are in need of guidance, it's important that you know what advice to give, so…

Take a betel leaf and pinch one side slightly to make a very shallow cone shape. Put a small amount of each ingredient into the cone and top with a little of the sauce. Fold over the excess leaf to close the parcel up, open wide, and shove it in! I have found that taking a small, polite bite from the parcel nearly always results in all the ingredients arranging themselves down the front of my shirt, so frankly I suggest going for the all-in-one approach, but it's up to you.

People presume that, because I am a chef, my children are somehow genetically programmed to enjoy all types of culinary delights, including those from the vegetable patch. Well, it's not true! I have suffered the same dramas as most parents in getting my pesky kids to eat 'one a day,' let alone five. For a long time I considered only three methods of persuasion:

1. Bribery. Eat your greens and I will give you dessert. This does work, but also means making industrial amounts of dessert.

2. Threat of punishment. If you don't eat your greens, I will drop a brick on your iPad. I like this option, but my wife, an elementary school teacher, says it's negative and counterproductive.

3. Fear. If you don't eat your greens, all your hair will drop out, your skin will become scaly, and your teeth will turn brown. This method stopped working when one child pointed out that this was a near-perfect description of Grandpa, and he does, in fact, enjoy vegetables.

It was my (annoyingly) sensible wife who suggested a fourth option—make vegetables taste very good! So here's my children's favorite vegetable dish. Okay, it does involve frying, so it's not a perfect everyday choice, but as an occasional snack it's a big hit.

I tend to use long-stemmed broccoli. I think the stem is the best part and should never be wasted, particularly if you grow your own. What the crunchy battered broccoli really needs is a clean-tasting yogurt dip. This one is based on the sort you get with your poppadoms in an Indian restaurant and is so versatile—I make gallons and use it with loads of different things. Anything cooked quickly in a tempura batter is best done at the last minute, so it's important to have everything ready, including serving dishes and dip, before you start cooking.

Ginger beer-battered broccoli tempura with minted mango yogurt dipping sauce

SERVES 4 AS AN APPETIZER OR TRENDY SNACK!

2 cups tempura flour

2 cups ginger ale or ginger beer, chilled

2 quarts vegetable oil, for frying

10oz broccolini

FOR THE YOGURT DIP

2½ cups Greek yogurt

½ mango chutney

2 tablespoons mint sauce (ready-made is fine)

We will start with the dip. Spoon your yogurt into a large bowl and stir in the mango chutney and mint sauce. If the chutney contains large pieces of mango, you may wish to chop it up a little before stirring in. Right, the dip is done! (By the way, this will make plenty, so chill what's left over and buy some poppadoms.)

Pour the flour into a mixing bowl and pour in the ginger ale or ginger beer while gently whisking. Don't overwhisk the batter: a few small lumps will merely make it seem more authentic and crunchy.

Pour the oil into a large, heavy-bottomed casserole pot and heat to 325°F. (If you don't own a thermometer, I'd advise asking for one for your birthday, but as a very rustic alternative you could check the temperature by dropping in a small piece of white bread. If it sizzles and goes a golden-brown color, you are good to go.) Dip the broccoli into the batter one stem at a time, turning to make sure each stem is well coated. Allow any excess batter to drip off before carefully placing the broccoli into the hot oil. Allow to sizzle for a few seconds before gently stirring the oil to make sure the broccoli stems do not stick together. When golden-brown, carefully remove the broccoli using a slotted spoon and drain on paper towels. Serve immediately alongside the dip.

66 Italy is not a country that immediately springs to mind when discussing spicy food. Chopped chile turns up on the occasional pizza, and chile oil is sometimes used to dress a salad, but it's not standard issue. So this dish is already very slightly brave with its use of fresh, fiery green peppercorns, but the really clever thing is that they are balanced with chilled sweet melon. Fresh green peppercorns are not always easy to find, though Asian supermarkets do often have them. If you can't get them, look for a can of green peppercorns in brine.

Now, I should confess that I was not clever enough to think up this perfect combination all by myself! I was served this risotto at a tiny restaurant halfway up a mountain while visiting Le Marche in Central Eastern Italy. The risotto was served after the appetizer as a prelude to the main course—a course called *primo piatto* in Italian. We hadn't ordered it; it just arrived! It was one of those occasions when you approach a meal with no high expectations at all (I was simply very hungry), and leave the table very slightly humbled by the sheer brilliance of what you have just been served. 99

Fennel risotto with chilled melon & green peppercorns

SERVES 4 AS AN APPETIZER (OR DOUBLE UP FOR A MAIN COURSE)

¼ really ripe orange-fleshed melon, such as cantaloupe

10 tablespoons unsalted butter, roughly diced

1 small onion, finely chopped

2 garlic cloves, finely chopped

sprig of thyme, leaves only

½ fennel bulb, very finely diced

¾ cup risotto rice (Arborio, Baldo, or my favorite, Carnaroli)

1¾ cups hot vegetable stock (it's fine by me to use a stock cube!)

2 tablespoons fresh green peppercorns

good pinch of salt

1 tablespoon freshly grated Parmesan cheese

The very first thing to do is peel the melon and cut the flesh into ½-inch cubes, then stick it in a bowl in the fridge until just before serving—the melon needs to be really cold when added to the risotto because this gives a wonderful heat contrast.

Melt the butter in a heavy-bottomed saucepan and add the onion, garlic, thyme leaves, and fennel. Cook gently until the vegetables are slightly softened and sizzling in the butter, but not colored at all. Add the rice, stir and cook for around 2 minutes (it's important to control the temperature so that the rice and vegetables do not color).

Add the stock, a ladleful at a time—it needs to be added bit by bit and you must stir continuously. Stirring is an important maneuver for the risotto maker because it causes the rice grains to rub and release starch, and this means you will end up with a good, creamy risotto.

I figure you will need most if not all of the stock. However, after 15–18 minutes of adding, stirring, and simmering, taste the risotto and if you are happy with the texture, it's time to move on to the final stage.

Reduce the heat to the bare minimum and stir in the peppercorns and salt. Make sure all risotto eaters are sitting down ready for their meal, then stir in the Parmesan and finally the chilled melon. An arugula and red onion salad dressed with extra-virgin olive oil would be great with this if serving as a main course.

66 A traditional Andalucían gazpacho is, of course, a chilled soup made using tomatoes as a base along with other vegetables and herbs found in that part of the world. It's a fine soup and in no need of any customization or modernization by me or any other food writer. However, unless there is some obscure law that I've not been made aware of, I am allowed to steal the word 'gazpacho' and use it to describe my own chilled soup.

Watermelon is a funny old fruit. I don't much care for a wedge of watermelon, but used in a salad with salty feta, perhaps, or in a soup such as this gazpacho, it works very well. We tend to think of gazpacho as a soup eaten at the beginning of a meal; however, in Spanish bars it is often served from a pitcher as a drink, which is how I recommend serving my version. Make up a batch of watermelon gazpacho and serve it in frozen shot glasses (perhaps with a sneaky glug of vodka!) either before your meal or on the side with a spicy dish. The gazpacho is best served as fresh as possible, but do leave enough time to chill it thoroughly in the fridge. If you are going to serve this in glasses, pop them in the freezer before you get going so they are super-cold and frosty-looking when required. 99

Watermelon, mint & chile gazpacho

MAKES ENOUGH TO FILL 16 SHOT GLASSES

1⅔ lbs watermelon chunks

1 large tomato

20 mint leaves

2 tablespoons peeled and chopped fresh ginger

2 red chiles, chopped

Remove as many seeds as you can from the watermelon and roughly dice the flesh. Chuck it into a bowl, then roughly dice the tomato and add to the watermelon. Add the mint leaves, ginger, and chiles.

Now all that remains is to convert your bowl of prepped ingredients into a liquid. I think this is best done in a food processor rather than a blender as a food processor will leave a little texture, which is nice, while a blender will process everything to a super-smooth consistency (as is a blender's purpose in life—I'm not complaining, just saying!). So tip your ingredients into a food processor and process to a fairly smooth but still textured soup.

Have a taste—you should pick out the watermelon as the overriding flavor, but there should be just a hint of acidity from the tomato, a background minty note, and of course a slight smack of chile. Apologies if I sound like a fancy sommelier describing a wine that's going to cost you a month's salary. If more mint or chile is required, pound a little more in a mortar and pestle and stir through the gazpacho.

Chill the gazpacho in the fridge until really cold, then decant into shot glasses and serve.

Cucumber, avocado & yogurt soup with fresh peach, ginger & fennel seeds

SERVES 6

pinch of fennel seeds

2-inch of fresh ginger, peeled

1 avocado, peeled, pitted,
    and roughly chopped

1 cucumber, peeled
    and roughly chopped

2 very ripe peaches, pitted and
    roughly chopped

½ cup Greek yogurt

juice of ½ lime

5 mint leaves, roughly torn

1 ripe plum tomato, roughly chopped

1 teaspoon sumac

1 cup water

¾ cup coconut milk

½ teaspoon salt

FOR THE GARNISHES

2 red chiles, finely diced

½ cucumber, finely diced

1 sweet, ripe peach, pitted and
    finely diced

1 tablespoon fennel seeds, ground

12 mint leaves, thinly sliced

2 teaspoons sumac

This soup makes a fantastic appetizer on a balmy evening—you could even serve it in shot glasses alongside another spicy appetizer. I've split the ingredients into two sections—the first is for the soup itself and the second is for all the garnishes that are stirred into the soup just before serving. A great way to serve the soup is with the garnishes in bowls to let people customize their own soup.

To make the soup, grind the fennel seeds to a powder in a mortar and pestle and set aside. Grate the ginger and then press it through a fine strainer over a bowl to extract as much juice as possible. Keep the juice and throw away the pulp. Put the fennel seeds and ginger into a blender and add all the remaining soup ingredients (I just about manage to get all this done in one batch in my blender, but if yours seems a little small, it's fine to do it in a couple of batches). Blend until smooth and then pour the soup into a container and shove it in the fridge.

Just before serving, prepare all the garnishes and either stir them into the soup (if you don't trust your family and friends to share fairly!) or put them in bowls on the table so that people can add as much or as little of each as they wish.

A few years ago my son was asked at school what his favorite food in the whole wide world was, and he replied, 'My Mom's pea soup.' When I was told this by his teacher, I obliged by laughing, as expected, and saying something like, 'Yes, well, it is very good,' before going home and smashing his PlayStation with a mallet. I wasn't only upset because he had chosen something Mom made instead of me—I can forgive a child that young for ignoring my culinary endorsement by countless food critics (including Michelin). No, it wasn't just that. I was upset because actually Mom's pea soup isn't that great to start with. She doesn't season her soup, she puts in way too much potato, and she cooks it for so long that it ends up a sort of khaki color. This pea soup is in another league, I guarantee. But I'm not bitter and it's all forgotten now...

This recipe is for 3 lbs of yellow split peas – freeze what you don't need in freezer bags (I put 2 servings per bag). I make most of my soups in larger quantities than required so that I can have a ready supply of soup at all times. Unfortunately so does my wife. I should also say that this soup could easily be made with dried lentils of any color in place of the dried peas.

Spiced yellow split pea soup

MAKES AT LEAST 20 PORTIONS

½ cup vegetable oil

1 onion, finely chopped

3 garlic cloves, finely chopped

2-inch piece of fresh ginger, peeled and grated

1 large tomato, roughly chopped

2 celery ribs, roughly chopped

1 medium carrot, roughly chopped

3 teaspoons ground cumin

2 teaspoons red pepper flakes

2 teaspoons garam masala

1½ teaspoons ground coriander

2 teaspoons fennel seeds

seeds from 5 cardamom pods

1 heaping tablespoon salt

3 lbs dried yellow split peas

chopped cilantro, to serve (optional)

Heat the oil in a large pot (the dried peas will swell during cooking—as will lentils, if you're using them—so make sure you use a decent-sized pot). Add the onion, garlic, and ginger and cook gently until slightly colored for 3–4 minutes. Add the tomato, celery, and carrot and stir everything together for half a minute. Add the remaining ingredients except the dried split peas and cilantro, stir, and leave to sizzle away for a minute or so.

Add the dried split peas (I never soak them prior to soup production, by the way) along with 5 quarts water and bring to a simmer. Cook for 35 minutes or until the peas are swollen and soft—the kitchen should smell good, too.

You now need to blend the soup to the desired consistency. I like my soup to have plenty of texture, so I use an immersion blender, which I randomly plunge in and blend until I get the desired effect. You can enjoy your soup just as it is; however, if you have your son's teacher around for lunch, you may like to go the extra mile and stir in some chopped cilantro before serving.

❝ I had this soup in a roadside café in the middle of nowhere in rural Arizona. It's very quick and easy, and if this were a glossy magazine, it would definitely be called Pantry Soup. Editors of food magazines and producers of daytime TV cooking shows are crazy for food that can be produced without any shopping involved! Egg in a soup is not unusual—I've discovered poached eggs floating in all kinds of soups in the past—but a fried egg is less common. I'm imagining that there is a Spanish, or more likely Mexican, influence going on here, though it was actually served to me by a Native American.

Don't skip the fried bread—it's the ingredient that pulls everything together—and make sure you serve the yolk very runny and deliver advice on breaking the egg up within the soup before eating it. Finally, for any food magazine editors or daytime TV producers browsing this tome, I'm very happy to rename the soup 'No Stop-to-Shop Soup' if it gets this book some free marketing. ❞

Fried egg soup with smoked paprika & ground chile

SERVES 4

3 tablespoons olive oil

2 garlic cloves, crushed to a paste

2 plum tomatoes, finely diced

1 teaspoon smoked paprika

pinch of salt

½ teaspoon red pepper flakes, ground to a powder

3 cups chicken stock (homemade would be fantastic, but if you've got a cube in that pantry...)

4 thick slices of white bread

4 free-range eggs

3 scallions, green parts only, thinly sliced

Heat 1 tablespoon of the olive oil in large pan and cook the garlic for 1 minute until very slightly browned. Add the tomatoes and simmer for about 2 minutes until softened and much of the juice has reduced. Stir in the paprika, salt, and ground red pepper flakes. Pour in the stock and bring to a simmer, then leave the soup to cook while you get on with the next step.

Heat another tablespoon of the olive oil in a frying pan and cook the slices of bread on both sides until golden and crispy. Tear them in half and put a half into each serving bowl. The other halves will be served on the side.

Add the remaining olive oil to the frying pan and fry the eggs until slightly under-cooked (they will continue cooking in the hot soup). Put a fried egg into each bowl on top of the bread, and pour on the hot soup. Sprinkle with the scallions and serve.

66 This book sets out to inform, inspire, and entertain in equal measure. Occasionally I may even dare to be controversial, but I have no wish to provoke a major international diplomatic incident, so I need to make it clear right here and now that this soup could be from Vietnam, the Philippines, Thailand, China, or even Cambodia. I'm not issuing it a passport; I'm just hoping you cook it and give it a try. As recipe titles go, this one is textbook-perfect. It contains seafood, it's spicy hot and soured with lime juice. What I love about this soup is the purity of flavor—it feels cleansing. The soup should be made just before serving and if you taste it at its various stages, you will notice the layers of flavor as they build up.

Now, this recipe is more of a list of suggestions than a set of rules. I firmly believe that chicken stock works better as a base stock for this soup than (the possibly more obvious) fish stock. You are welcome to experiment. Whichever you choose will present you with your next decision... do you make a fresh stock or go with a store-bought cube? I go for the compromise solution. I simmer 5 cups of stock made with a cube and throw in 6 chicken wings to give it a bit of body. Chicken wings are really cheap. After simmering the wings for 20 minutes, I fish them out and give them to the cat—I keep the stock. Right, so your stock is simmering and your guests are ready to eat; now begins the hot and then the souring process.

Another decision concerns the shrimp. To get maximum flavor from the shrimp, you must cook them whole, unpeeled, heads and all. Let your guests peel them or, do as I do, eat everything bar the head, which you can throw out. If your guests are the timid type, it's probably worth peeling them. It's your call. 99

Hot & sour seafood broth

ENOUGH TO CLEANSE 4 SOULS

5 cups chicken stock (see intro)

6 chicken wings (optional)

2–3 red bird's eye chiles

8 kaffir lime leaves

2 lemongrass stalks, each cut into 3

$\frac{1}{3}$ cup fresh peeled and sliced ginger

$\frac{1}{3}$ cup palm sugar

8 shiitake mushrooms, sliced

1 raw squid tube, sliced into rings

8 raw large shrimp in the shell

splash of fish sauce

juice of 2 limes

$\frac{1}{3}$ cup cilantro, very roughly chopped

Make up the stock using my suggestion above, or as you see fit, and bring to a simmer in a large pan. Pound 2 of the chiles with the lime leaves, lemongrass, and ginger in a mortar and pestle. Don't pound to a paste, but bash it up well. Tip into the simmering stock and stir.

Add the palm sugar—if it's in cake form, grate it into the stock; if it's a liquid, simply spoon it in. Taste the broth (as it is now known)—it should have a punch from the chiles but you should also pick out a sweetness from the sugar as well as lots of flavor from the ginger, lemongrass, and lime leaves. Don't expect any sourness, as we haven't done that part yet! So... here's another decision: if you think the broth could be hotter, bash the third chile and throw it in. My view is that this soup needs to be fiery hot but you can overrule that if you like, since I'll never know!

Right, back at the stove ... add in the sliced shiitake mushrooms, squid rings, and shrimp—they will all be cooked and ready in 4 minutes, so keep going. Add a splash (that's about 2 teaspoons to the pedant) of fish sauce to give a slightly musty, Asian flavor—and it negates the need for any salt, by the way—and add the lime juice. Stir in the cilantro and take a taste. Is it spicy? Sweet? Aromatic? Sour? Good, that's checked all the boxes. Ladle it into soup bowls, making sure everyone gets equal amounts of shrimp, squid, and mushrooms.

Last Tuesday one of my staff cleared out the freezer. As a standalone fact, this may not impress you that much. Perhaps you have a good knowledge of food safety and hygiene and you were presuming that we should be cleaning our freezer every Tuesday as a matter of course, which I assure you we do… I merely mention it in passing, because it led to a culinary discovery of epic proportions.

Part of the job of cleaning the freezer is to compile a list of any stuff found lurking for which there appears to be no obvious use. These are the things that make a chef his money. Find useless stuff, create a dish, give it a French name, double the price and *voilà*! A business plan is born. On the list last Tuesday was 4 pounds of shrimp shells. They weren't labeled raw or cooked, which would have been helpful. However, since they were a dull gray as opposed to a pinky-orange color (foolishly called "Lobster-red" by one paint company—foolish because we all know that lobsters are a beautiful blue-black color), we knew that they must have been the shells of raw shrimp, peeled and served on a previous menu.

One of my chefs suggested that we use them to make the classic French soup, bisque. I was all for this. (French name…double the price—are you thinking what I'm thinking…?) Bisque is a rich shellfish soup often thickened with rice. Traditionally the shellfish used, be it shrimp, crab, or lobster, are inferior specimens that would not sell at the market, or indeed the shells of said shellfish, such as those found in our freezer. So I commissioned a bisque to be made with our shrimp shells, at which point one of my other chefs said that it might be a good idea to veer away from the classic French recipe, and instead use coconut milk as the stock and infuse a little chile and lemongrass for extra flavor. I love to see that sort of inspirational creativity springing from the mind of one of my chefs. Better still, when it happens in private so that I can claim the inspirational idea as my own, but unfortunately on this occasion the idea was witnessed and shared by all those gathered around the now neatly stacked and labeled freezer.

I am not a man who considers himself a fusionist guru simply through adding lemongrass and chile to a classic French dish—that kind of innovation is lazy and often results in a clash of culture and flavor. However, sometimes it just works, so I give you Shrimp & Coconut Bisque.

Shrimp & coconut bisque

SERVES 6 GENEROUSLY

⅓ cup olive oil

2 lbs shrimp shells (see note below)

½ fennel, roughly diced

1 carrot, roughly chopped

1 tomato, cut into 8 wedges

½ onion, roughly chopped

4 garlic cloves, roughly chopped

pinch of saffron

1 star anise

2 heaping tablespoons risotto rice

3 x 14oz cans of coconut milk

2½–3½ cups water

1 heaping teaspoon salt

3 red bird's eye chiles

4 lemongrass stalks

¾ cup peeled and sliced fresh ginger

15 lime leaves

First, heat the olive oil in a large pot over a high heat. Add the shrimp shells and cook fiercely for about 3 minutes or until they take on a pinkish color and give off a lightly roasted aroma. Reduce the heat and add the fennel, carrot, tomato, onion, and garlic. Cook gently for 2 minutes, then add the saffron, star anise, and rice.

Pour in the coconut milk and 2½ cups of the water and bring to a simmer. Cook for 30 minutes or until the rice grains are soft and swollen. Pour the soup, shells and all, into a blender and blend until smooth.

Strain the soup to remove any fibrous bits and then return to the pan. At this point you should have a rich-tasting shellfish soup with a creamy coconut flavor lurking in the background. If you feel it is a little thick, add some or all of the remaining water. Add the salt in stages and taste as you go.

Heat the soup back to a simmer. Bash the chiles, lemongrass, ginger, and lime leaves in a mortar and pestle and add to the soup, stirring well. Simmer for 2 minutes and only then remove from the heat and leave to cool. This short simmering with the chile, lemongrass, ginger, and lime leaf keeps the fresh flavor of these aromas alive, while the slow cooling ensures maximum infusion. Reheat the soup and serve with grilled naan bread or store in the fridge or freezer to enjoy later.

A SHORT NOTE ON OBTAINING SHRIMP SHELLS

The easiest way to lay your hands on shrimp shells is to buy whole, fresh, unprepared shrimp and choose a dish that requires peeled shrimp. (You won't believe this, but such a dish can be found—Shrimp Pappardelle with Chile, Lemon, Garlic, Basil & Parsley on page 122. You may need to eat this dish more than once in order to obtain 2 lbs shells, but that's no hardship, believe me.)

Once you have peeled the raw shrimp, wrap up the shells and stuff them in the freezer. If you are the type that goes in for a bit of high-end cooking, you may, from time to time, end up with crab or lobster shells. Keep these, too, because bisque can be made from a variety of shells, both cooked and raw.

The title may contain two words that you are not that familiar with, so I shall explain. Tilapia are fish native to East Africa, and are farmed extensively. They are herbivorous fish, which in ethical terms is a good thing, and they taste great, which in culinary terms is also a good thing. They are perfect to use for an escabeche, but that's no help to you yet, because I haven't explained what that is…

An escabeche is a dish made with fried fish, which is then marinated in a sweet-and-sour liquid. It has been around for many years, turning up in English cookbooks as far back as the seventeenth century. It's thought to have Spanish origins, but many cuisines have a similar dish. I guess originally the purpose of the sweet-and-sour liquid was as a preservative.

So, now we are all up to speed, I need to tell you a story. I started my career at the Ritz Hotel in London during the 'last hurrah' of nouvelle cuisine. Food had to be delicate and very, very pretty. I spent hours pouring aspic over carefully cut vegetables and shaping seahorses out of puff pastry. I learned a lot, but it was my next job that changed everything for me. I went to work at Le Soufflé restaurant near London's Hyde Park Corner for a chef called Peter Kromberg. He was a born leader and a fantastic cook. All these years later I am certain that he was the greatest influence on me, my career and my approach to cooking. He taught me to taste food, he mocked my efforts at fancy plates and encouraged me to compromise prettiness at the expense of flavor. This is his escabeche recipe, and it proves a point—it has a huge flavor!

Tilapia escabeche

SERVES 6

5 tablespoons olive oil

8oz tilapia fillet

½ small fennel bulb, cut into very fine strips

1 large carrot, cut into very fine strips (us chef types call this julienne)

1 onion, thinly sliced

1 garlic clove, finely chopped

2 tablespoons white wine or cider vinegar

⅔ cup water

2 sprigs of fresh thyme

2 tablespoons chopped cilantro

pinch of ground coriander

2 star anise, halved

small pinch of saffron

pinch of cayenne pepper

2 teaspoons sugar

pinch of salt and twist of pepper

lettuce leaves, to serve

The first thing to do is cook the fish. Heat 1 tablespoon of the oil in a hot frying pan and add the fish, skin-side down. Fry for 2 minutes or until the skin has colored a little. Transfer the fish to a ceramic or porcelain dish, laying it skin-side down, and set aside at room temperature. (The fish will not be cooked through at this point. The rest of the "cooking" process happens when it comes into contact with the pickling vegetables.)

Heat the remaining oil in a pan and add the fennel, carrot, onion, and garlic. Cook for 3 minutes or until softened but not colored. Pour in the vinegar and water and bring to a boil.

Add all of the remaining ingredients except for the lettuce leaves and stir for 30 seconds. Remove the pan from the heat and spoon the mixture over the fish—make sure you get a good even spread of all the bits and liquid. Cover the dish with plastic wrap and puncture a few holes in the top. Leave to cool at room temperature, then transfer to the fridge and leave well alone for 24 hours.

Before eating your escabeche, take it out of the fridge at least 1 hour before serving, to let things warm up slightly. Place the tilapia onto a serving plate and put a small pile of the vegetables on top. Trickle on some of the juice from the dish and serve at room temperature with a few lettuce leaves.

66 This is a quirky yet useful recipe. Quirky because cakes should be sweet and made with fruit or chocolate and definitely cream, not stuffed full of olives, spices, and cheese; useful because it is a really quick, simple and tasty alternative to homemade bread. You can knock this up in under an hour minus all the hassle of breadmaking. It's great served warm with unsalted butter, just as you would a fresh loaf of bread, or serve it with sliced charcuterie or a smoked fish pâté, or topped with a salad of beets, watercress, and goat cheese. 99

Savory cheese & olive cake with chile & smoked paprika

MAKES 1 LOAF

4 free-range eggs

⅔ cup dry white wine

⅔ cup olive oil

2 cups all-purpose flour

1 teaspoon baking powder

1 teaspoon smoked paprika

pinch of red pepper flakes

pinch of salt

1 cup pitted green olives, drained and each one sliced into 3 rings

1 cup sun-dried tomatoes in oil, drained if very oily

1¼ cups grated mature Cheddar, (any hard cheese would work)

I usually make this in an electric mixer but the process is exactly the same and almost as quick by hand.

Mix the eggs, wine, and oil—the beater attachment of the mixer is best, or use a wooden spoon if making by hand. Add the flour, baking powder, smoked paprika, red pepper flakes, and salt and again beat the mixture enough to incorporate everything.

Fold in the olives, tomatoes, and grated cheese by hand. Bake in a lined loaf pan at 325°F for 45 minutes. Allow to cool in the pan for 10 minutes and then turn out onto a wire rack for another 10 minutes to cool.

Serve while fresh and warm or store in an airtight container for up to 3 days and warm gently before serving.

❝ Everyone loves crispy phyllo shrimp, right? But how often have you been offered homemade ones? Well, the reason for that is they are, admittedly, a tiny bit fussy to make, but don't let that put you off trying them. The good news is that they can be made well ahead of time when you've got a quiet and empty kitchen available.

White radish is sometimes called mooli or daikon, but it's the same thing and fairly widely available in most supermarkets. It's important to tell you that the world's heaviest daikon weighed over 70 lbs. That's a whopper, and luckily you don't require one that big. ❞

Crispy phyllo shrimp with white radish & soy chile dipping sauce

MAKES 12 WRAPPED SHRIMP, IDEAL FOR 4

1 small white radish

2 carrots

10oz phyllo dough

12 raw peeled large shrimp

2 red chiles, thinly sliced

1 tablespoon coarsely chopped cilantro

1 free-range egg, beaten, mixed with 2 tablespoons cold water

vegetable oil, for frying

FOR THE SOY CHILE DIPPING SAUCE

1 tablespoon sweet chile sauce

1 tablespoon soy sauce

good pinch of red pepper flakes

juice of 1 lime

1 tablespoon sesame oil

PHYLLO OBSERVATIONS

The first thing to note is that phyllo dough is a tricky customer. Shop around and experiment until you find the brand that works best for you. Once you've opened the package of phyllo, you should lay all the sheets on a baking sheet, cover the top sheet with a cloth, and store it in the fridge. Use the phyllo, sheet by sheet, straight from the fridge.

But before we even open the package of phyllo, we must cut the vegetables. Cut the white radish and carrot into julienne strips the same length as the shrimp. A mandolin is a great tool for this job, but otherwise it's down to your knife skills!

Cut a strip from a sheet of phyllo about 4 inches long and 1 inch wider than the shrimp. Lay a shrimp at one end of the phyllo strip (it's worth making a small incision in the curved back of each shrimp so that you can push the shrimp flat) and arrange a small pile each of the white radish, carrot, chile, and cilantro alongside the shrimp.

Lightly brush the exposed phyllo with the beaten egg and water, fold the excess over either end of the shrimp and then roll up until the shrimp and vegetables are encased. Wrap all the shrimp in this way and either cook straight away or store them on wax paper in the fridge for up to 3 hours, if you wish.

To make the dipping sauce, simply mix the ingredients together in a bowl.

Heat some vegetable oil in a large, deep frying pan—the level of the oil should be deep enough to allow the shrimp to float. Cook the shrimp, in batches if needed, turning a couple of times, until golden brown and crispy on all sides. Remove using a slotted spoon and drain on paper towels for a few seconds before transferring to a plate. Serve with the dipping sauce.

There's just so much to tell you about this dish. First, we need to discuss the term 'potted,' which refers to a method of food preservation popular in medieval times. The pot was actually a heavy, flour-based, inedible pie shell made specifically for holding food, rather than for eating.

Many types of food—such as eels, lampreys, pigeon, pork, and countless other delicacies—were cooked and then decanted into these pie crusts along with melted butter. Once the butter had set and the pie was sealed, the food within would last much longer, allowing for transportation. Over time the pie shell was replaced by a dish or pot, but with very much the same purpose.

In Britain, brown shrimp were stored this way. They would have been processed and potted where they were caught, which would probably have been Morecambe Bay in Lancashire, an area long associated with the small brown shrimp (or *Crangon crangon*, in case any marine biologists are tuned in) used in potted shrimp. Mace and nutmeg were commonly used 'back then' as flavorings, and for me the spicy butter is one of the most appealing parts of the whole dish, particularly when balanced with the liveliness of dill and the sharpness of lemon.

I love this dish. We serve it in the restaurant on toast and that is how I'm going to suggest you make it. If you want to put the mixture into a ramekin, that's fine by me (do so at the point where I suggest getting your plastic wrap out); however, I think this way actually makes life easier.

I should have mentioned above, but forgot in all the excitement of my history lesson, to tip you off about brown shrimp purchasing. Raw brown shrimp have a brown shell, but if you're buying cooked and peeled ones, they will be a dusky pink color. Don't confuse them with the Norwegian type used in a shrimp cocktail—brown shrimp are much smaller. If you ask your fishmonger, he should be able to get hold of them.

Potted shrimp with nutmeg & mace

SERVES 4 AS A GENEROUS APPETIZER OR LIGHT LUNCH

8oz cooked and peeled
 small shrimp

about 20 ice cubes

2½ cups cold water

9 tablespoons unsalted butter

1 shallot, finely chopped

pinch of sea salt flakes

1 heaping tablespoon chopped
 fresh dill

grated zest of 1 and juice of ½ lemon

generous pinch each of ground mace,
 cayenne pepper, and grated
 nutmeg

the best whole-wheat bread
 you can find

watercress salad, to serve

Tip the shrimp into a large glass or metal bowl, then tip the ice cubes into an even larger bowl and pour in the cold water (if you don't have a bowl large enough to hold the ice cubes and water, improvise—use a large pan, or even the kitchen sink). Place the bowl containing the shrimp into the iced-water bowl.

Put the butter, shallot, and salt into a pan over low heat and gently melt the butter (on no account should you allow it to burn or color). Remove from the heat and leave to cool for 3 minutes, then pour the melted butter mixture over the shrimp.

Stir gently using a spoon or spatula as the ice cools the butter, which will eventually harden and set. It's important to keep everything moving so that the butter sets evenly rather than against the cold edges of the bowl. While stirring, add the dill, lemon zest and juice, mace, cayenne pepper, and nutmeg. Keep stirring until the mixture loses its liquidity and starts to thicken.

Get your plastic wrap out! Lay a sheet of plastic wrap about 20 inches long on the work surface. Spoon the shrimp and butter mixture onto the plastic wrap and use your hands to work it into a large sausage shape around 3 inches in diameter. Roll the shrimp up in the plastic wrap and tie at either end. Chill in the fridge. Your shrimp "sausage" will need at least 3 hours in the fridge to set completely.

Do whatever you like during this time—it's no business of mine ...

When you are ready to serve, turn on your broiler, cut 4 slices from the whole-wheat loaf, and toast them on both sides. Remove the shrimp "sausage" from the plastic wrap and cut into 4 generous slices about an inch thick. Place 1 slice onto each piece of toast and squish them a bit to cover the toast evenly. Place the toast back under the broiler until the butter just begins to melt. Don't leave for too long—2 minutes should do it. Serve immediately with a watercress salad.

Scallops are certainly not a cheap meal option. Furthermore, the best scallops (for eating, and for the environment) are hand-dived, which are unfortunately more expensive still. So this dish is one you'll probably make infrequently and save for when you are entertaining friends, rather than sitting in front of the TV with a tray on your lap! I first tried this in Thailand and loved the purity of it. Simple flavors merely 'upselling' the key ingredient.

The freshest scallops are those sold in the shell, meaning they could well still be alive when you buy them. I have given a free tutorial on opening a scallop shell just in case it seems a little daunting. If scallops are not your thing, or you struggle to find any really nice ones, you could use thinly sliced sea bass or even salmon.

A quick word about the tomatoes. If you are the type of person who dashes around the supermarket at a hundred miles an hour paying little or no attention to what us chefs call 'considered sourcing,' hold on. Really ripe, sweet, red tomatoes are key to this dish. Rummage through what's on offer and select the very best available. The tomato water is best made a day in advance, if possible.

OPENING SCALLOPS IN THE SHELL

A scallop is a bivalve, meaning it has two shells. The upper shell is fairly flat while the lower shell is concave and holds the meat. Always store scallops in the shell with the flat shell uppermost. As scallops are an expensive ingredient, you want to extract as much of the meat as possible and an offset spatula is the best tool for the job. Lay the scallop on a work surface with the flat shell uppermost. Carefully work the offset spatula inside the crack between the two shells and run it across the inside of the flat shell, ensuring the spatula stays flush with the top shell, releasing it entirely.

You will now be eyeball to eyeball with a scallop. The meat we want is the large white muscle. Scoop the offset spatula under this muscle to release it completely.

The shells can be thrown away or given to friends as ashtrays (they will be really pleased!).

Gently pull the orange coral away from the scallop—you can pan-fry the corals and have them as a cook's treat for lunch tomorrow. You are now left with the large white meaty scallop and some frilly gunky nonsense that we call "the skirt." Pull away the skirt and discard it. *Voilà*, one glorious scallop. Once you've prepped all of your scallops they can sit happily in a container in the fridge for a few hours.

Raw scallops with tomato water, fresh ginger & lemongrass

SERVES 4

8 large diver-caught scallops, removed
from the shell (see opposite)

1 avocado, peeled, pitted, and diced
into ½-inch cubes

½ cucumber, halved, seeded, and
diced into ½-inch cubes

a few small lettuce leaves, such as
frisée lettuce, lamb's lettuce,
and fancy cresses

20 salted peanuts

pinch of red pepper flakes

1 tablespoon sugar

1 tablespoon Crispy Shallots
(see page 186, or buy ready-made
from Asian supermarkets)

FOR THE TOMATO WATER

6 really ripe plum tomatoes

4 lemongrass stalks

2-inch piece fresh ginger

2 red bird's eye chiles,
finely chopped

1 tablespoon sugar

½ teaspoon salt

A large square of clean cheesecloth
is very useful

Right, now to the actual dish. The first thing to make is the tomato water—
I would do this the day before if possible. Bring a pan of water to a boil
and have a bowl of cold water close by. Remove the eye from the tomatoes
(the eye is where the stalk joins) and plunge the tomatoes into a boiling
water for 10 seconds. Carefully remove them from the boiling water using
a slotted spoon and plunge them into the cold water to halt the cooking
process. Peel away the skins and discard, then roughly chop the tomato
flesh and throw it into a bowl. Blanching the tomatoes in this way helps to
increase the resulting yield of tomato juice.

Cut each lemongrass stalk into 3 lengths and bash with a rolling pin, then
toss into the bowl with the tomato flesh. Grate the ginger (don't bother
peeling it) and add that to the bowl as well. Add the chiles and stir in
the sugar and the salt. Now pour everything in the bowl into a blender or
food processor and blend it all up for about 30 seconds.

Place a large square of cheesecloth in a clean bowl and pour in the pulp.
Tie up the cheesecloth and let it hang over the bowl to drip until all the
tomato water has come through—a couple of hours. I do this in the fridge.
Every now and then give the cheesecloth bag an encouraging squeeze. This
should produce about 2 cups of tomato water, which you should then chill.

To serve the dish, take your scallops, slice each one into 4 disks and arrange
on four serving plates. I usually go for a simple line of scallops, each one
slightly overlapping the next. Dot the cubes of avocado and cucumber
randomly across the plates, and do the same with the salad leaves.

Bash the peanuts, red pepper flakes, sugar, and Crispy Shallots in a mortar
and pestle until they resemble coarse bread crumbs. Serve the scallops
with a bowl of crunchy shallot and peanut crumb on the table for people to
add themselves. Finally pour your pungent tomato water into a pitcher and
ask your butler to pour a little over each person's scallops.

> If there were a Crispy Squid Eating World Championship, I would be remortgaging my house and putting all my money on my son, Richie, to come home with the gold medal. Crispy squid is one of those snacks that translates into any language. Spanish, Italian, Greek, Thai, Indian, Chinese...they all have a version. Some years ago I was stationed on the crispy squid section of a buffet catering for some incredibly posh guests at a well-to-do private party. Toward the end of lunch, a lady in a stupidly large hat glided past my station and told me that the food had been divine (I hate that word as a culinary description), apart from the onion rings, which were chewy and tasted peculiar. I just smiled.
>
> The key to frying squid is to have the oil nice and hot, so the squid cooks very quickly. A hand-held thermometer is useful to indicate the temperature of the oil, but remember the temperature will continue to rise if the oil is left on the stove! The usual way of frying squid is to first coat it in either a batter or a seasoned flour. Batter is great but quite messy, so I opt for the simpler seasoned flour approach.

Salt & pepper squid with papaya, chile & cilantro salsa

SERVES 8 AS AN APPETIZER OR 4 FOR LUNCH

2¾ cups all-purpose flour

2 tablespoons smoked paprika

1 tablespoon salt

2 tablespoons cracked black pepper

vegetable oil, for frying

12 raw squid tubes, cleaned and cut into 1-inch rings, and tentacles (see opposite)

FOR THE SALSA

1 papaya, finely diced

1 small red onion, finely chopped

1 small red pepper, seeded and finely diced

1 red chile, finely diced

grated zest and juice of 1 lime

10 mint leaves, finely chopped

a bunch of cilantro, finely shredded (stems and all)

1-inch piece of fresh ginger, grated

2 tablespoons sweet chile sauce

2 tablespoons olive oil

First make the salsa. Mix all of the ingredients and leave to stand at room temperature for 1 hour (not you, the salsa!).

Meanwhile, mix the flour with the paprika, salt, and pepper on a large plate or dish. Pour the oil into a deep-fryer or large pan deep enough to hold 2 inches of oil. Bear in mind that it will bubble up when you put the squid in, so allow for this and don't overfill the pan. Heat the oil to 350°F.

The squid should be floured just before it's fried, so just before the oil reaches the required temperature, toss the squid thoroughly in the seasoned flour and shake to remove any excess. Working in small, manageable batches rather than throwing it all in at once, gently slide the squid into the hot oil and let fry for about 4 minutes or until lightly colored. Cooking too much at once will cause the oil temperature to drop considerably, which in turn means that the squid takes longer to cook and therefore ends up chewy, so cooking in batches is really important here.

Carefully remove the crispy squid from the oil using a slotted spoon, drain on paper towels, and serve immediately with the salsa.

A NOTE ON BUYING AND CHOPPING SQUID

On page 12 you will find a short piece of advice on maintaining an ethical approach to purchasing fish—this applies to squid, too, so do read it. Most of us choose our friends based on emotional attachment; however, if you're honest, you may have collected a couple of friends based on good old practical grounds. Some people befriend a mechanic, or an electrician. Plumbers have loads of friends, and some very clever foodie types make sure that their local fishmonger loves them just enough to be of great value when they are buying fish. Fresh fish is always best, and if you can befriend your fishmonger, he will always tell you what is seasonal and fresh, rather than selling you what he might have to throw out the next day (it happens). You may even be able to develop your relationship to a point where you can call the fishmonger up, tell him what you'd like

to cook, and he'll pick it up from his suppliers. He may well ask what size you'd like. Ask for squid with a body about 6–8 inches long—that will give you a decent-sized squid ring.

There's no point in chatting up a fishmonger and then not putting it to good use, so I'd ask him (yes, yes, or her) to prep the stuff. Ask them to give you skinned and cleaned squid tubes (the main body) and also the tentacles. As an appetizer portion I would work on 1½ tubes per person, and a few bonus tentacles. Before frying your squid, place the tubes on a cutting board and, using a sharp knife, cut them into rings about an inch wide. There are various shapes you can cut squid into before frying, but for this chunky dip I suggest rings are best because you can squeeze and hold the salsa in the squid ring. Clever, eh?

A word on chiles & which to buy for each recipe

ABBREVIATED HISTORY

Records show that, in Mexico, wild chiles were being gathered and eaten by 8,400BCC (before Christopher Columbus). The Spaniards and Portuguese took them to India and South East Asia, and from there they traveled to the Middle East. By the sixteenth century chiles were being enjoyed throughout Europe.

TYPES OF CHILE

Cayenne, habanero, jalapeño, scotch bonnet, naga, tabasco, and bird's eye are just a few of the many types of chiles. Which varieties are available to you will depend very much on where your cooking takes place geographically. When writing this book I had originally decided to be very chile-specific, but my local selection of supermarkets tend to stock just two varieties, so I decided to stick with what's most readily available:

1. The standard red and green chile (variety unspecified) is about 4 inches long with smooth skin. These chiles are flavorsome but never mind-blowingly hot, so I've tended to use them in recipes that require a good visual presence or in dishes that are more subtly spiced.

2. Bird's eye chiles, both red and green, are used in many of the recipes. They are much smaller than our standard friends above, about 2 inches long, and the skin is slightly wrinkled. The bird's eye chile is not to be underestimated—it punches well above its weight in terms of spiciness.

Chiles are always hot and spicy; this is the result of years of natural selection. The fiery kick of the cunning old chile will deter any animal from returning for a second bite … apart from one animal, that is. For some reason humans quite enjoy chomping on really hot chiles, and farmers throughout time have cross-fertilized and genetically selected their seed crop to produce ever more hot and fiery ones. Various studies and much research have been done by biologists, psychologists, and inebriated young men eating in Indian restaurants into how much chile can be consumed, and indeed why we enjoy the sensation in the first place. Though not conclusive, the "benign masochism" theory seems to be the popular explanation, meaning that we enjoy the thrill of the chile burn because we know that ultimately it can do us no harm. If this book represents your first steps into the world of spicy cuisine, exercise a little caution. All of the recipes that use chile work well as far as my taste buds are concerned, but feel free to cut down the quantity if you feel I may be further down the road to culinary masochism than you.

In the early twentieth century, a pharmacist called Wilbur Scoville devised a sort of chile league table. Each variety was assessed and awarded "heat units" to show which were the hottest of all. The table has had various league leaders as chile growers crossbreed in search of ever hotter varieties. One little trick worth noting is this—the hottest part of the chile is the white membrane, or placenta, that attaches the seeds to the flesh. By removing this membrane you will reduce the net impact of the chile substantially. It's a good trick when you require the visual abundance of chile minus the total heat. I often finish a dish with a salad of cilantro, toasted coconut, and red chile sliced finely on an angle. I remove the seeds and membrane from the chiles so that I can use more chile for a greater visual impact.

Cooking with chiles can also be hazardous. Cutting boards should be scrubbed well after chile preparation, or whatever you chop next will be exposed to the juice of the chile. Always wash your hands thoroughly after chopping chiles and refrain from rubbing your eyes, your nose, or indeed any other body part that could be sensitive to the sting of chile. A good cook should, of course, refrain from any type of bodily rubbing (of themselves or anyone else) until the apron is off and they've left the kitchen, but that's just good old health and safety.

Sea trout ceviche with lime & vanilla dressing, lotus root chips & soy beans

---

SERVES 4

1 lb skinless ocean trout (or salmon)

½ tablespoon salt

½ tablespoon sugar

FOR THE LIME & VANILLA DRESSING

grated zest and juice of 2 limes

1 teaspoon wasabi paste

good pinch of sea salt flakes

2 vanilla pods

⅔ cup extra-virgin olive oil

FOR THE LOTUS ROOT CHIPS
& SOY BEANS

approximately 40 frozen soy beans
    (edamame)

1 lotus root bulb

1 cup vegetable oil

TO SERVE

kejap manis (see page 75)

salad leaves or cress (optional)

PREPARING THE SEA TROUT

If at all possible, buy your trout on the day you intend to eat it to ensure it is as fresh as possible. Lay the trout fillet in a large dish and sprinkle with the salt and sugar. Chill the fish in the fridge for 2 hours, during which time it will release a little moisture. This process, known to intelligent types as osmosis, will change the texture of the fish very slightly, making it both easier to slice and more pleasing to eat. After 2 hours, wipe the top of the fish with a clean cloth to remove any excess moisture, salt, and sugar.

Now, using a very sharp knife, cut the fish across the fillet into very thin slices. You should end up with at least 20 slices. Lay the trout onto 4 serving plates, cover with plastic wrap, and refrigerate for 2–3 hours.

MAKING THE DRESSING

The dressing can be made a few hours, or even a day, in advance and chilled until needed. Simply whisk well shortly before using. Put the lime zest and juice into a bowl and whisk in the wasabi paste and sea salt flakes. Split both vanilla pods and scrape the seeds into the bowl. Add the olive oil and whisk again to incorporate thoroughly.

THE EDAMAME

If using podded edamame, all you need to do is defrost them before use. If you are using beans still in their pods, defrost a few about 10 minutes before and then pop out the required number of beans.

THE LOTUS ROOT CHIPS

The lotus root chips can be prepared up to 4 hours in advance. Take the lotus root bulb and slice very finely—this is definitely a job for your Japanese mandolin!

Heat the oil in a small high-sided pan until it reaches 325°F and then put in the lotus root. Allow it to sizzle away until golden brown and crispy. Remove from the oil using a slotted spoon and drain on some paper towels. Store in a dry place until needed (and don't forget to take the pot of oil off the heat!). Finally tip a little of the kejap manis into a small bowl and have a teaspoon handy.

SERVING

When you are ready to serve, remove the plates of sliced fish from the fridge and remove the plastic wrap. Give the dressing a final whisk, then paint it generously over the fish using a pastry brush, reserving a little of the dressing. Dot the edamame over the fish and top with the lotus root chips—I like to lay the chips against each other so that they stand up. Drizzle the reserved dressing around the fish. Last, dip the tip of a teaspoon into the kejap manis and allow it to drip over the fish—don't add too much! If you wish, you can add a small salad leaf or a sprinkling of cress to finish the dish.

WASABI

A number of years ago, I had a Japanese student come to work as part of my kitchen team for a few months. She went home over Christmas and on her return to the UK she knocked on the office door and told me she had brought me a special gift back from Japan. I was very excited, thinking it would be some incredibly expensive high-tech electronic gadget bought in Tokyo, and was a little bemused when I noticed that the gift had been wrapped in damp tissue paper. It turned out to be fresh wasabi, a root grown in water. Most of us will struggle to find fresh wasabi, but luckily it can be bought as a paste or as a powder to which water can be added. It's often called Japanese horseradish. A botanist would point out that it's not a relation of horseradish at all, but the cook would counter that by telling the botanist that the flavor does indeed resemble horseradish. Most people's wasabi education probably begins in a sushi bar where it's offered as a simple paste alongside raw fish, but it can also be used in sauces, pickles, marinades, and dressings.

66 This is one of my favorite recipes in the entire book. First, I think it's fabulous to eat, which is obviously a basic requirement when creating a dish, but I also like its purity—clean, healthy flavors with more than a passing nod to Japanese cuisine. We often put this on the menu at The Victoria and it always proves an immensely popular appetizer. I also make it at home. It's not really a Tuesday evening supper dish as it requires a little more effort than I can be bothered with on a weekday evening, but when friends come over it makes the perfect appetizer.

This dish also goes some way to demonstrating how I create a recipe in the first place. Shamefully I have had very few original ideas at all. Some chefs just seem able to start the creative process from scratch, which I admire greatly, but that's not me. I'm a plagiarizer. Interpreter more than thief, I hope. I see an idea in another chef's restaurant, hijack it, and then set about tearing it apart and rebuilding it to a point where I think I can claim custody.

Some years ago I had the great fortune to be sent to New York with someone else's credit card. Fantastic! I was booked to do a few cooking demonstrations each day, but by night I was free to roam the Big Apple in search of culinary excellence. Along with a good friend and fellow chef, I headed off to many of New York's finest ~~strip clubs~~ culinary establishments and ate some terrific food. On the last night, after a foodie conversation with an in-the-know New York concierge, we were encouraged to try out Jean-Georges Vongerichten's latest restaurant at that time, Spice Market, situated in the Meatpacking District. It was the best meal of the trip for me, by far. I've returned to the restaurant several times since and always leave thinking that this could well be my favorite restaurant in the world. The décor is exotic: high ceilings, low tables, cool lighting, and lots of carved wood (all of which remind me of Zanzibar in many ways), with great New York service, and the food is sensational.

On that first occasion we were served a dish of finely sliced, very fresh raw salmon, and on one part of the plate was a spicy, crispy onion 'crumb' that we sprinkled over the salmon. There was also a sweet and sharp pickly thing on the plate which I can't quite recall, but the dish was stunning. I knew right then that I was going to use it as inspiration for one of my own back home, and here is that dish. 99

Salmon "sashimi" with shallot & chile crunch & pickled cucumber

SERVES 4

1 lb skinless salmon fillet

2 teaspoons salt

2 teaspoons sugar

1½oz tube wasabi paste

5 tablespoons Shallot Crunch
(see page 186)

1 batch Asian Cucumber Pickle
(see page 189)

12 Lotus Root Chips
(see pages 50–51)

12 tablespoons kejap manis

First "cure" the salmon using the salt and sugar to withdraw moisture, leaving the flesh of the fish slightly firmer with a meaty texture, and also making it a little easier to work with. Scientific types call this process osmosis. Place the salmon on a large plate or dish, skin-side down (or where the skin once was, because I told you to remove it—just testing!). Mix the salt and sugar together and sprinkle evenly over the salmon piece. Cover with plastic wrap and chill in the fridge for at least 3 hours.

Remove the salmon from the fridge and wipe it with a paper towel or a clean, damp cloth to remove the excess salt and sugar. Transfer the salmon to a cutting board. The piece of salmon is bigger than the 4 portions

CONTINUED... ⟶

Salmon "sashimi" with shallot & chile crunch & pickled cucumber

CONTINUED FROM PAGE 53

required, so we can trim the fish to get a really good shape, which is so important in Japanese cooking. Remove a strip of salmon about an inch wide from the thinnest side of the fillet, which will leave you with a fillet that is narrower but of a more even depth. Stick the scraps in the freezer and use it to make fishcakes next week, or give it to the cat.

Find the wasabi and a brush and paint the top of the fillet of salmon with a generous spread of wasabi paste. Pour the Shallot Crunch into a large dish and lay the salmon, wasabi-painted-side down, on top of the shallots. The wasabi will help "glue" the Shallot Crunch to the salmon. Turn the salmon over and place on a clean cutting board. You should now be looking at a large chunk of salmon with an even spread of crunchy shallots over the top, forming a thin crust.

Using a sharp straight-bladed knife, cut thin slices across the salmon fillet. Lay the slices onto 4 serving plates, add a good dollop of the Asian Cucumber Pickle to each slice, and top with a Lotus Root Chip. Drizzle a little kejap manis over each plate using the tip of a teaspoon and serve immediately.

AN APOLOGY

I get frustrated when a food writer keeps referring to recipes on other pages, making what seemed like a simple recipe much harder and more complicated. I've tried to limit that maneuver in this book in case it upsets you, too, but this dish has caught me out. Both the Asian Cucumber Pickle and the Shallot Crunch can be made well in advance.

A NOTE ON SALMON

Not all salmon is the same. For a start, there is wild salmon and farmed salmon. Wild salmon tastes fantastic but is scarce and expensive, so I tend to use a farmed variety.

Look for salmon from a named farm. Most supermarkets and fishmongers will stock a top-end farmed salmon, and often it's organic, but not always. As we are essentially serving raw fish here, freshness is paramount. Don't use frozen salmon for this dish. When buying your salmon, ask for a piece from the head end of the fillet, as the flesh there is thicker and more suitable for this recipe. Ask for the skin to be removed, too. Finally, take care when handling the salmon—if the flesh tears in any way, it will ruin the look of the finished dish.

"I have a speech reserved for family visits to our local Chinese restaurant. I won't bore you with the full 18-minute version, but it begins, 'Of course, kids, this isn't real Chinese food. Oh no. If we were in China we'd be eating...' and then I come out with a list of ingredients that sound like Hannibal Lecter's shopping list, in order to demonstrate how un-Chinese our experience actually is. The truth is I've no idea, because I've never actually been to China. My kids invariably inform me that they don't care how Chinese the restaurant's menu is, 'And can we order some shrimp toast now?'

I love shrimp toast, or Hatosie as it's known locally. I expect that shrimp toast is a rather silly fast-food treat to those in the know, but it's one of my guilty pleasures. Actually, that whole guilty pleasure thing is a bit pathetic. People never actually reveal their deepest guilty pleasures. If I enjoyed smoking crack while wearing Speedos and listening to Supertramp, now that really would be a truly guilty pleasure, and not one I'd ever consider putting in a book. For the record, my top five printable guilty pleasures are:

1 . . . . Shrimp toast (dipped in sweet chile mayo)
2 . . . . The Carpenters' greatest hits
3 . . . . Spitting out chewing gum and trying to volley it over a fence
4 . . . . A mesh shirt on a cold day
5 . . . . .Cheddar cheese and strawberry jam sandwiches on white bread "

Shrimp sesame toast

SERVES 4

FOR THE SHRIMP TOAST

15 raw peeled large shrimp (keep the shells for the Shrimp and Coconut Bisque on page 35)

2 scallions, thinly sliced

1 red bird's eye chile, finely chopped

about 10 cilantro leaves

2 free-range egg whites

2 teaspoons soy sauce

pinch of salt

2 teaspoons cornstarch

4 slices white bread

2 teaspoons sesame seeds (a mix of black and white is nice)

2 cups vegetable oil

A Stupidly Simple Dip (see page 193), to serve

Put the peeled shrimp into a food processor along with the scallions, chile, cilantro leaves, egg whites, soy sauce, salt, and cornstarch. Process it to a coarse paste and spread thickly and evenly onto the bread slices. Sprinkle with the sesame seeds and either chill in the fridge for up to 3 hours or cook immediately.

When you are ready to cook, heat the vegetable oil to 325°F in a pan that allows the oil to be at least 3 inches deep. Lay the bread into the oil shrimp-side down (you may need to fry the bread one slice at a time, depending on the size of your pan). The bread should start to sizzle right away. Cook for 2 minutes, then turn it over and give it another minute or so. Carefully lift the toasts out of the pan and drain on paper towels.

Cut the toasts into either fingers or mini triangles—this is completely up to you. I leave the crusts on, but if your friends are posher than mine (very likely), you don't have to. Serve with the Stupidly Simple Dip.

Author's note: If any young children are browsing this book, I have never smoked crack and would not encourage anyone to do so. If any middle-aged men are browsing this book—Speedos? Just don't! If anyone of my age is browsing this book, ain't nothing wrong with Supertramp!

In Zanzibar, enterprising street-food sellers convert their bicycles into barbecues with pedals. They cycle these machines into Stone Town and fire up the coals. Most of the delicacies come on a skewer, and my favorite is this spicy chicken version. Now, I'm not sure if I have the exact recipe—in fact I suspect the original recipe may change according to what's available—but back home I set about recreating what I'd eaten and I figure it's almost as good. And, no, I haven't converted my bicycle...yet.

These skewers are ideal for a barbecue, or you can cook them indoors in a grill pan or a non-stick frying pan. I am merely suggesting that you serve these with Mango & Red Pepper Jam and a few Plantain chips, but if you like these suggestions see pages 192 and 187 respectively. The first thing to do is visit your butcher and ask him to grind the chicken breast for you. You could chop the chicken by hand—and in Zanzibar I bet they do—but frankly, life's too short.

Spiced chicken skewers with plantain chips, mango & red pepper jam

MAKES 20 SKEWERS (4 WOULD SATISFY A VERY HUNGRY, MILDLY GREEDY PERSON!)

30 cashew nuts

2 lbs chicken breast, ground

2 free-range eggs

4 teaspoons ground cumin

½ teaspoon salt

3 teaspoons chile powder

2 tablespoons vegetable oil

1 tablespoon fresh white bread crumbs

4 teaspoons very finely grated ginger

1⅓ cups cilantro leaves, finely chopped

3 teaspoons garam masala

1 onion, very finely chopped

1 teaspoon white pepper

Soak 20 wooden skewers in warm water to prevent them from burning (particularly important if you intend to barbecue the skewers). Next assemble all the ingredients. I grind the cashew nuts in a mortar and pestle until they resemble bread crumbs.

Put the ground chicken breast in a bowl. Whisk the eggs with the cumin, salt, chile powder, and oil and add to the chicken. Mix to combine, then add in the bread crumbs, cashew nuts, ginger, cilantro, garam masala, onion, and white pepper. Mix it all up and divide into 20 lumps.

Roll each lump into a sausage shape and thread a skewer through the center so that you have a "sausage" of spicy chicken at one end of the skewer. These can be left in the fridge until required.

When you're ready, simply take a few skewers and cook, in batches if necessary, on a barbecue or in a grill pan or non-stick frying pan over high heat for about 8 minutes, or until cooked through, turning occasionally. If you're cooking them in batches, keep the cooked ones warm in the oven but don't leave them unguarded because they smell fantastic and someone will steal one!

This could very easily have ended up in the Simple Supper Spice chapter, but it makes a good appetizer or snack, too, so it's staying put. If by chance you ever invite me over for dinner, you may wish to know that my favorite roast is slow-roasted pork belly (must have plenty of apple sauce), and if in the unlikely event I leave before it's all finished, this is what you must make the next day. Of course, you might prefer roast beef, but that shouldn't prevent you from enjoying this salad, so I've given an easy roasting method.

Pork belly is wonderful because it's so fatty and the fat packs all the flavor. Because it's fatty, it's generally paired up with something tart, such as the aforementioned apple sauce, or in this case pineapple. The pineapple could be thrown in completely raw and you would still have a very reasonable salad, but oven-drying or dehydrating changes the texture and intensifies the flavor. You are also taking tentative steps into the world of high-end molecular gastronomy, which will give us something to discuss if I do come over for dinner because I know nothing about high-end molecular gastronomy and I'm eager to learn! Finally, a quick heads-up on the dressing. It's a very important part of the salad and is definitely best warmed through before serving to really release all of the flavors.

Salad of pork belly, oven-dried pineapple & shiitake mushrooms

SERVES 4

1⅓ lbs boneless pork belly

2 teaspoons salt

4 decent slices from a sweet, ripe pineapple

olive oil, for frying

about 12 shiitake mushrooms, thickly sliced

2 Boston lettuces, each cut into 6–8 wedges

10 long sprigs of cilantro

12 stems broccolini, cooked and cooled

If your pork is raw, you will need to cook and cool it before the salad fest. If using precooked leftovers, skip the cooking part and simply cut the pork into bite-sized chunks.

Preheat the oven to 325°F. Place the pork skin-side up on a baking sheet and rub the salt into the skin. Cook for an hour, or until the meat is tender and has a lovely roasted color. Don't panic if the skin hasn't crisped up—it isn't necessary at this stage. Leave the pork to cool, then cut into bite-sized chunks.

The pineapple also needs a little while in the oven but unfortunately at a different temperature from the pork, so you'll need to cook them separately. Sorry about that. Remove the skin from the pineapple slices and cut each one into about 12 wedges. Place a wire rack on a baking sheet and spread the pineapple out on the rack. The very best way of cooking the pineapple would be to leave it in the oven overnight on the very lowest possible temperature— at the restaurant we do this on the oven pilot light. Second best is setting your oven at 125–200°F and giving the pineapple about 2 hours. Keep an eye on it, because we don't want it to color. It should wither and dry but

FOR THE DRESSING

1 teaspoon black bean paste

2 teaspoons cracked black pepper

pinch of red pepper flakes

1 tablespoon soy sauce

2½ tablespoons sweet chile sauce

1½ teaspoons white wine vinegar

juice of 1 lime

¼ cup sugar

¼ cup peeled and grated fresh ginger

2 tablespoons water

2 garlic cloves, finely chopped

¼ cup olive oil

remain yellow. It will be chewy and a little shrivelled and basically dried when ready. It can be stored for a day or two in the fridge if not immediately used.

With these things done, you are ready to go.

Heat a frying pan and add a touch of oil. Add the pork belly chunks and cook them for about 5 minutes or until brown and crisp. Transfer them to a bowl. Cook the mushrooms until caramelized and add these to the pork. Add the lettuce wedges, cilantro, broccolini, and pineapple.

Heat all the dressing ingredients together in a small pan until just warmed (but not hot), spoon over the salad and serve.

MACE & NUTMEG

These both come from the same plant—the nutmeg tree. Hanging from the tree is the nutmeg fruit, which are far less commonly available than mace or nutmeg themselves. At the heart of the fruit is the nutmeg, and woven around the nutmeg is the mace. Both are usually bought dried and separate from one another, and both are widely used in both sweet and savory dishes. Incidentally, you may have read that nutmeg is capable of producing a "high"—back in my college days myself and two friends smoked my mom's entire supply of ground nutmeg, and absolutely nothing happened at all. Well, that's not strictly true—I was grounded for a month, but we didn't get high. It does turn out that the information had some basis of truth, but frankly it's not a reason for buying it!

I certainly don't want to give the impression that this section is all about dinner-party food. Personally, I have every reason to discourage dinner parties because I think you should go to a (my) restaurant on special occasions, always eating the full three courses (plus cheese), and choosing only the finest (expensive) wines. No, this section is about dishes that could be part of a bigger, more extravagant meal, but are equally fine being served up and eaten as they come. Contrary to many modern food writers, I believe that most cooks actually enjoy cooking, and so the following pages contain some dishes which require a bit of hard work, but don't let that put you off. I'm with you all the way and have tried to indicate how you can chop some of the recipes down into stages and prepare parts in advance, thus making the cooking times seem a little less like hard work! Many of these dishes require nothing else to serve alongside; however, a few may ask you to detour to other parts of the book where a suitable suggested addition is given in more detail.

Spicing up your lunch & dinner

> Laksa is usually classified as a soup, but it's not a lightweight affair suitable only as an appetizer. A laksa is a meal in itself—that's certainly how I serve it. Chinese-Malay in origin, laksa comes in various styles, forms, and flavors. This version is known as a curry laksa. The defining features of a laksa are the rice noodles, the tofu, the laksa paste, and the coconut sauce. Now I confess I used to be a bit anti-tofu. I always gave it a wide berth, considering it some sort of odd, bland, diet-conscious vegetarian substance. In a way, it is all of those things, but it's also much more than that. Fried into puffs, it takes on a great texture and being rather subtle- (not bland)-tasting it absorbs other flavors extremely well. Fried tofu puffs (or curd puffs) can be bought ready made, but if you can't find them, buy a block of tofu, cut it into cubes, and deep-fry it until golden brown.

Butternut & tofu laksa

SERVES 4

3 cups (12oz) bean sprouts

2 heads bok choy, coarsely shredded

1/3 cup unsalted peanuts

2 tablespoons vegetable oil

1/2 butternut squash, diced into
    1-inch cubes

2 1/2 cups coconut milk

1 1/4 cups water

20 curry leaves

1 tablespoon sugar

good pinch of salt

6oz dried white rice noodles

8oz fried tofu puffs

about 20 basil leaves, ripped and torn

about 15 mint leaves, ripped and torn

about 30 cilantro leaves,
    ripped and torn

3 limes

FOR THE LAKSA PASTE

3 large red chiles

2 banana shallots, chopped

1/4 cup peeled and chopped ginger

2 garlic cloves, chopped

1 teaspoon curry powder

1–2 tablespoons water

First make the laksa paste. Place all of the paste ingredients into a food processor and blend to a smooth paste. Set aside in the fridge.

Both the bean sprouts and the bok choy would be best precooked. Bring a small pan of water to a boil and toss in the bean sprouts. Stir them around for 30 seconds and then fish them out with a slotted spoon and dunk them into a bowl of cold water to halt the cooking process. Then do exactly the same with the shredded bok choy. Drain the bean sprouts and bok choy and keep in the fridge for now.

Heat a frying pan over medium heat and toss in the peanuts. Let them color slightly all over, leave to cool and then coarsely crush them in a mortar and pestle. Set aside. Add 1 tablespoon oil to the frying pan and cook the butternut squash until just softened and golden-colored all over—7–8 minutes.

Place a wok over the biggest heat source on your stovetop and add the remaining vegetable oil. Tip in the laksa paste and cook gently for 5 minutes, stirring occasionally. Pour in the coconut milk and the water and bring to a simmer. Bash up the curry leaves in your mortar and pestle and toss these into the wok. Add the sugar and salt.

Put the noodles into a bowl and pour on enough boiling water to cover them. Allow them to steep for 3–4 minutes before draining. The noodles will be translucent and soft.

Now find your serving bowls—I suggest wide, shallow bowls, allowing you to see all of the different elements in the soup. Divide the noodles among the four bowls. Scatter the tofu into the bowls. Now back to the actual soup in the wok. The next part must all happen very quickly—within a minute: chuck in the squash, the bean sprouts, bok choy, and half the amount of each herb. Halve the limes and squeeze in all the juice. Place a squeezed lime half in each person's bowl. Pour the hot soup over the noodles and tofu in the bowls. Scatter in the peanuts and the remaining herbs and serve.

66 Several years ago I was aboard a small 12-person plane bound for Zanzibar. This was my first trip back to the island as an adult. As we approached the tiny dot in the Indian Ocean, I could feel a strong sense of 'belonging' to this exotic island. I was born in 1967 in Dar-es-Salaam, the capital of Tanzania. I would have been born in Zanzibar, but there had been a revolution on the island a couple of years before and as a result the hospitals were still in a state of disarray. Back in Zanzibar we lived in a big white house with three floors and a fabulous veranda overlooking the crystal-clear waters that surround the island, and Stone Town, the center of the island's capital, was only a short walk away.

My dad was a marine biologist stationed at the East African Marine Fisheries Organization. My mom had stopped work to care for what she rightly believed to be the most charming, beautiful baby ever born. We lived on Zanzibar only for a short while after my birth, but the island remained a very special place to our family and I felt a strong urge to return and explore the place as an adult. My cooking has been very much affected by our time abroad. Spice is the prevailing theme in Zanzibar, but how each spice is used depends on one's personal heritage— Persian, Arabic, Chinese, African, and Indian foods are all common and reflect a very colorful history. Each time I have cooked a spicy dish on TV or for a magazine, I have always mentioned Zanzibar in glowing terms.

The island's population is tiny and the list of inhabitants who have gone on to achieve any level of fame is very small. In fact I come in second, just behind Freddie Mercury, which shows you just how short the list is! So it did cross my mind that news of my constant 'upselling' of this fabulous place may have filtered back to the Zanzibari authorities, and that I would probably be driven from the airport to Stone Town in a cavalcade with gunmen firing volleys of celebration into the air. As it happened, they arranged a completely different surprise reception. They sent a local taxi driver who cunningly managed to take a 32-mile version of the 7-mile journey to Stone Town and stripped me of most of my vacation money before I'd even arrived.

Although the island's cuisine is multinational, the list of ingredients isn't huge. This is a small island in the middle of the Indian Ocean, after all. Fish plays a big part, and each day dhow boats leave the shore, returning hours later with an array of amazing species. Another ingredient that is hard to miss is coconut, and of course spices are everywhere. Zanzibar's biggest export is cloves. This dish is not a very precise Zanzibar recipe. It is my take on a dish we ate time and again and I've loosely based it on one my mother makes called 'kuku aku paku,' or chicken in coconut milk. The choice of fish is up to you—I have made some suggestions, but the sauce is the important part. I would suggest serving this with sticky rice and a salad. 99

Zanzibar-style fish curry

SERVES 4–6   RECIPE OVERLEAF   ⟶

Zanzibar-style fish curry

CONTINUED FROM PAGE 65

1 whole fish, about 1 lb,
    (mullet, bass, bream, or tilapia
    would all work well), scaled
    and gutted

1 lb mussels in the shell

12 raw large shrimp in the shell

2½ teaspoons cumin seeds

2 teaspoons coriander seeds

6 cardamom pods, outer husks
    removed

2 cloves

½ teaspoon ground turmeric

vegetable oil, for cooking

2 large onions, very finely chopped

5 garlic cloves, very finely chopped

2-inch piece of fresh ginger,
    peeled and grated

3 green bird's eye chiles,
    2 thinly sliced into rings
    and 1 left whole

4 medium tomatoes, very finely diced

3⅓ cups coconut milk

⅔ cup chicken or fish stock

juice of ½ lime

small bunch of basil

pinch of salt (optional)

Chill the fish, mussels, and shrimp in the fridge while you prepare the sauce. Grind the cumin seeds, coriander seeds, cardamom, and cloves to a fine powder in a mortar and pestle. Add the ground turmeric and set aside.

Heat a glug of vegetable oil in a large pot over medium heat. Add the onions, garlic, ginger, and the sliced chiles (leave the whole one for now). Cook for 1 minute, stirring. Add the tomatoes and sizzle for 1 minute. Add the spice mix and pour in the coconut milk and the stock.

Bring to a simmer and cook for about 20 minutes or until slightly thickened. At this stage you could cool and refrigerate the sauce for a couple of days, then reheat it when you are ready to cook the fish, or just proceed straight to the finish line.

Take the whole fish out of the fridge and chop off its head. Cut the body into 4 large, even chunks, cutting straight through the bone. Add the fish chunks, mussels, and shrimp to the simmering sauce and cook for around 6 minutes or until the fish lifts away from the bone easily, the mussels have opened, and the shrimp are pink.

Grind the whole chile in a mortar and pestle and add to the pan. Squeeze in the lime juice, tear up the basil and stir into the curry. Taste and add the salt if necessary. Serve immediately.

This dish would work very well with sea bass, sea bream, large mullet, or snapper. As a guide, a 1-lb whole fish would generously feed two people. Ask your fishmonger to prepare the fish for you—he needs to scale it, trim off the fins, and remove the guts. As with all fish, insist that it's as fresh as possible. Buy it on the day you intend to eat it if you can.

" This is a fantastic dish both to cook and to eat, but before we go any further we need to clear up one small issue—whole fish have bones. I say this because we occasionally cook a whole fish at the restaurant and every time we do, you can guarantee that someone will summon the waiter and inform him that there is a problem with the whole fish we have just served.

'Excuse me, waiter, this whole baked bass has bones in it.'

'Er, right, yes, I'll take it back to the kitchen.'

'Chef, table 4 says there are bones in this fish.'

'You don't say. It's a whole fish—of course it's got bones in it!'

'But what shall I tell him?'

'Tell him if he can catch one without bones, I'll cook it for free.'

Okay, rant over.

A whole baked fish with a funky broth on the side looks pretty darn impressive, but is actually very simple and straightforward. You have options on the type of fish you can use (see left), and if it's a fish you've caught yourself (or if you can get away with fibbing), the dish becomes more impressive still. The broth served with the fish was inspired by a dish I had cooked for me (I say me; there were about 70 people in the restaurant, but you know what I mean) by a very highly regarded American chef famous for his Mexican-inspired cuisine. Making the broth is interesting because you will taste the layers of flavor stacking up as each ingredient is added.

The fish can be marinated ahead of time and kept in the fridge until required. It will take around about 30 minutes to cook in the oven and should be served right away (rather than have it sit around while your guests make light work of your finest gin and the green olives you found in the pantry). The broth is best made and served immediately, so I would suggest getting all the broth ingredients ready well ahead of time, meaning you can prepare it while the fish bakes. "

Whole baked sea bass with wok-fried peppers & a citrus, chile & cilantro broth

SERVES 4

1 large or 2 small sea bass, about 2 lbs, scaled and gutted

olive oil, for roasting and drizzling

2 tablespoons oyster sauce

2 tablespoons soy sauce

4 teaspoons sugar

2 sprigs of thyme, leaves only, finely chopped

Begin by marinating the sea bass. Lay the fish on a cutting board and, using your sharpest knife, slash the fish five times on either side across the body to make shallow incisions deep. Have a large nonstick roasting pan at the ready, big enough for the fish but small enough to fit in your oven (I know it's obvious, but there will be someone…). Slosh a glug of the olive oil into the pan and spread evenly. Mix the oyster sauce, soy sauce, sugar, and thyme leaves together in a small bowl and spoon the mixture into the incisions, then put the fish into the pan. Drizzle a touch more olive oil over the fish and chill in the fridge until your guests have arrived. When you are ready to cook, preheat the oven to 325°F and cook the fish for 30 minutes for 1 large fish, or around 10 minutes if you are using 2 smaller fish.

MORE INGREDIENTS OVERLEAF …   CONTINUED OVERLEAF… ⟶

Whole baked sea bass with wok-fried peppers & a citrus, chile & cilantro broth

CONTINUED FROM PAGE 67

FOR THE CITRUS, CHILE &
CILANTRO BROTH

olive oil, for stir-frying

2 red peppers, seeded and
thinly sliced

2 yellow peppers, seeded and
thinly sliced

1 red chile, seeded and sliced
into very fine rings

1 green chile, seeded and sliced
into very fine rings

¾ cup peeled and grated fresh ginger

6 garlic cloves, finely chopped

1¾ cups fish or chicken stock
(I prefer to use chicken,
but it's your call)

grated zest of 1 orange and juice
to taste

grated zest of 1 lime and juice to taste

grated zest of 1 lemon and juice
to taste

1½ teaspoons sugar

pinch of salt

1 small bunch of cilantro,
finely shredded

That's really about it on the fish front except to say that in my professional world I would commission an eager chef to flip the fish over halfway through the cooking time, to make sure both sides benefited from the dry heat of the oven, whereas at home I'd think about it and then think "nahhh, it'll be ok." Your call.

Now for the broth. Bear in mind that you are possibly going to be cooking this in front of your guests, so hide this book (though do recommend it enthusiastically to them after dinner), look confident, and everything will be fine. Heat a good glug of olive oil in a wok over a high heat until nice and hot. Add the peppers and stir-fry for 1 minute until slightly softened but not colored. Add the chiles, ginger, and garlic and toss them around for a minute or two so they begin to cook. Pour in the stock and gently nudge everything down so they are fully submerged. Reduce the heat to medium-low and bring the stock to a gentle simmer. Have a taste—you will get the garlicky, gingery peppers and quite a distinct fishy flavor (if you are using fish stock) along with a good tingle from the chiles.

Add the citrus zest and stir, taste once again—you should now notice a real zing to the flavor—then add the sugar to give an important layer of sweetness (you can say all this out loud to your guests if you want—they'll be impressed!). Squeeze in the juice of half the orange, lemon, and lime and taste. If you want increased citrus, add more juice (I suspect you'll want a bit more, but maybe not all of the lemon juice). Add the salt, stir in the cilantro, and serve right away.

I suggest serving the broth in a big pot with a ladle and transferring the whole fish to a large serving dish and letting everyone scrape off its flesh and pour in their own broth. Spinach or green beans would do as a vegetable side, and if anyone mentions fish bones…

I'm indulging myself here, I admit. Many chefs, myself included, look back at dishes from five or ten years previously and cringe a little. It's a bit like flicking through your teenage record collection. But this particular dish has appeared at every restaurant I've been in charge of— it's adapted itself to each venue but essentially remains the same. I like it as much now as I did back then. Bass is the ideal fish for this dish because it can be cooked hard and fast in a hot pan. It's worth mentioning that wild bass is infinitely better than farmed, if you can get hold of it or happen to know a decent fisherman. This is more a set of directions for assembly rather than an actual recipe, so apologies in advance for the references to recipes on other pages, which makes cooking it a little more complicated. You could always pop into the restaurant and let me cook it for you.

Pan-fried sea bass on sag aloo & onion bhajis with curry oil & tomato chile jam

SERVES 4

1½ tablespoons vegetable oil

1 onion, finely chopped

1 tablespoon hot curry powder

1¼ cups olive oil

4 sea bass fillets, each about 6oz, cut in half

¾ cup plain yogurt

1 quantity Sag Aloo (see page 197)

1 quantity Onion Bhajis (see page 198)

1 quantity Tomato Chile Jam (see page 190)

First make a curry oil. Heat a frying pan over medium heat, add 1 tablespoon of the vegetable oil and cook the onion until golden brown, then mix in the curry powder. Pour in the olive oil and allow to simmer for 10 minutes. Remove from the heat and leave the infused oil to cool, stirring occasionally. Pass the oil through a fine sieve or some cheesecloth, then store the oil in the fridge until needed.

Heat a nonstick frying pan over high heat, add the remaining vegetable oil, and cook the sea bass fillets, skin-side down, until the skin colors slightly and starts to crisp up. Turn the fish over and cook a little more gently on the other side.

Fleck four plates with a little yogurt—the yogurt will add a nice mellow contrast to the stronger flavors. Warm up the sag aloo and spoon some into a ring mold (this is a very cheffy maneuver but we are replicating a restaurant dish here—otherwise, just place a few spoonfuls on the plate). Put a sea bass fillet on top of each portion of sag aloo.

Fry the onion bhajis and divide equally among the plates, placing them on top of the sea bass. Spoon a dollop of Tomato Chile Jam on top of the bhajis and drizzle a little infused curry oil around the plate.

You could of course simply cook the bass and serve all the other things on the side—it would taste just the same!

"Thailand, April 2011... so, take a fillet of bass (you could use bream, mullet, or even haddock, I guess) and cut it into 6 chunks. Toss the chunks in flour, throw them into hot oil and fry them (a Frenchman would weep to see bass deep-fried in this way!). When the fish is cooked, the outside should be crispy and the inside moist, hot, and sweet. Place the fish into a bowl with some wedges of really ripe tomato and a few cilantro leaves, and now the sucker punch—pour on a cold dressing made of fresh lime juice, fish sauce, crushed fresh mint, raw shallots, thinly sliced lemongrass, and chile paste.

I'm not sure if this is exactly what we ate last night, but through a sort-of conversation with a Thai restaurant owner involving quite a lot of mime, and good old detective work, I figure it's pretty close. It's also an excellent example of how I write most of my recipes. This recipe is being typed at 7am on a beautiful Thai island called Khol Khud, 150 miles from the mainland. Last night I went with my family around the coast in a speedboat and up a narrow inlet to a wooden shack on stilts where we sat at a low table on big cushions, watching the sun go down on one side while a cheerful Thai lady cooked with chile and a smile on the other. I knew right away that we were in for an incredible meal—one that would instantly rank in my top five dinners ever (I love a list). As yet I haven't made this dish, but from what I ate last night I know it's something I'm going to cook and eat again and again."

Fried fish with rice noodles, chile, lemongrass & fresh herbs

SERVES 4

1¼ cups vegetable oil

4 sea bream fillets, each cut into
    5–6 pieces across the fillet

handful of all-purpose flour

10oz straight-to-wok or precooked
    rice noodles

4 medium tomatoes, cut into 8 wedges

4 scallions, thinly sliced on
    an angle

⅓ medium cucumber, halved
    lengthwise, seeded and
    thinly sliced

1 banana shallot, thinly sliced
    into rings

2 Boston lettuces, cut into 8 wedges

3 tablespoons roughly chopped
    cilantro

2 tablespoons roughly chopped basil

10 mint leaves, roughly chopped

Crispy Shallots (see page 186),
    to serve

FOR THE DRESSING

½ lemongrass stalk, very thinly
    sliced into rings

2 tablespoons peeled and
    grated ginger

3 garlic cloves, roughly chopped

1–2 red bird's eye chiles, roughly
    chopped, seeds and all!

1½ tablespoons fish sauce

juice of 2 limes

1 tablespoon sugar

First, make the dressing, which can be done well before dinner and even a day or two in advance. Grind and pound the lemongrass, ginger, garlic, and chiles (with plenty of aggression) in a mortar and pestle until they form a coarse paste. Add the fish sauce, lime juice, and sugar and stir well. Have a taste—it should be powerfully spicy. Look for the individual flavors and redress the balance between hot, sweet, sour, and salty, if you feel the need, by adding a little extra of any of the ingredients. Dressing done.

The next bit is done "to order," as we professional types say. The best approach is to have all the ingredients prepared and ready to go.

Heat the oil in a pan. Use one that is deep enough to hold about 2 inches of oil with at least 3 inches of pan left above it, to allow for the frying, bubbling fish. Heat the oil until it's about 350°F (see the note on useful equipment on page 14). Toss the pieces of fish in the flour and shake off any excess. I recommend cooking the fish in two batches so the temperature of the oil stays nice and hot. Lower the first batch of fish into the pan using a slotted spoon—it should bubble and hiss in the hot oil right away. Allow to cook for 3–4 minutes until it is a little crusty and pale golden on the outside, then lay it on some paper towels. Repeat with the remaining fish.

The plan now is to mix the hot fish with the remaining ingredients and serve as quickly as possible, so don't answer the telephone or pour another glass of wine. Focus!

Place the noodles in a large, wide serving dish or bowl. Add the tomatoes, scallions, cucumber, shallot, lettuce, cilantro, basil, and mint. Place the fish on top. Pour on half the dressing and very gently turn everything over a couple of times to mix. Don't overwork it and be careful not to break up the fish.

Serve in bowls with the remaining dressing and Crispy Shallots on the side for people to add as they wish.

Steamed fish might sound a little drab but is actually a fabulous way of enjoying the real flavor of fish. Not all fish is perfect for steaming—oily fish such as mackerel, herring, or trout need that caramelization from a hot frying pan, I think, but halibut, sea bass, brill, turbot, and salmon can all be steamed very successfully. A quick word on halibut: if you can afford to use wild halibut, that is definitely the way to go, but a farmed version is available and usually considerably cheaper. Wild halibut can grow very large, so don't ask for 'one whole halibut, please,' or you could end up eating the same fish for a very long time… and have to sell the family silver to pay for it! Request your fish by weight—5–6oz of boneless halibut fillet per person is a generous portion. The best equipment for steaming fish is the Asian-style bamboo basket that sits on top of a pan of boiling water. Some cooks like to flavor the water with black beans, spices, herbs, or wines and vinegars—personally I don't think it makes any difference, but you're welcome to try. This dish feels vaguely Japanese to me—I'm certainly not saying it's authentic in any way, but there's a purity and simplicity of flavor that is of a Japanese style. 99

Steamed halibut with shrimp toast & green pea & wasabi purée

SERVES 4

2 slices of Shrimp Sesame Toast—
     (see page 55)

1 heaping cup frozen peas

up to 1oz wasabi paste

2/3 cup water

4 portions of halibut, each
     about 5–6oz

about a teaspoon of sea salt flakes

baby cress (optional
     cheffy customization)

1 tablespoon kejap manis
     (see opposite)

First of all, have a look at the shrimp toast recipe on page 55, just so you know what to buy and what the recipe entails. You could make your shrimp toast mix several hours in advance. The pea and wasabi purée can also be made and chilled and then reheated as required, so I shall start with that part of the recipe.

Bring a pan of water to a boil and toss in the peas. Let them simmer for 2 minutes and then pour them into a strainer and from there into your blender. Immediately start the blender working (we want to maintain the fantastic green color, so working quickly through the stages is important). Once the peas have blended for about 2 minutes, stop the machine and add the wasabi paste and the water before blending for another 2 minutes—this should leave you with a very smooth, very green purée with a fairly loose consistency. Have a taste: look for the sweetness of the peas but also the fiery kick of wasabi. If in doubt, add more wasabi—it's an important flavor in the overall dish. Add a little more water if you think the purée is too thick.

(If you choose to cool your pea purée for later use, pour it into a large container and shove it in the fridge to cool it down as quickly as possible. A microwave is the best way of reheating the purée.) So your purée is made and your shrimp toast mix is ready to spread on bread and fry, which means you are free to cook the fish when required.

Take a bamboo steamer basket and place your halibut portions inside, sprinkle with the flaked salt, and put the lid on the basket. Place the basket over a pan of simmering water. A snug fit will ensure that all the steam filters through into the basket. It's very difficult to say exactly how long your fish will steam for, but expect it to take 5–10 minutes.

Once it is ready, you should serve the halibut as soon as possible, so make sure that your shrimp toast is cooked, your pea purée is hot, and that you have the kejap manis close by. You are free to serve however you wish, but if a cheffy, plated version appeals, here's what I do: swipe the pea purée across each plate by putting a generous spoonful on one side of the plate and then dragging the spoon through the purée, drawing the purée across.

Place your shrimp toast across the purée and your bass on top of the shrimp toast. Sprinkle over a few cress leaves, if using, and finally trickle a little kejap manis from the tip of a spoon across the plate.

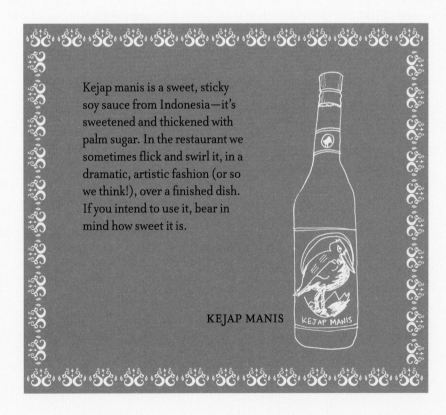

Kejap manis is a sweet, sticky soy sauce from Indonesia—it's sweetened and thickened with palm sugar. In the restaurant we sometimes flick and swirl it, in a dramatic, artistic fashion (or so we think!), over a finished dish. If you intend to use it, bear in mind how sweet it is.

KEJAP MANIS

In Britain, it's a long-accepted fact that a restaurateur can charge extra for any dish with a French word in the title. Chicken pithivier with *pomme purée* is worth so much more to the average customer than a simple chicken pie and mashed potatoes. Likewise, if one were to serve an apple tart with custard sauce, it would not have the same effect on gross profit as serving the very same apple tart with *crème anglaise*. I'm not sure this theory extends to other languages, but you'll note I slipped a little Spanish into the title in the hope that I may be able to nudge the price of the book northward a touch. It's worth a try in these tough economic times. This dish is a great one and well worth the price of the book alone. It's very easy to make and guaranteed to please. *Patatas bravas* are, very simply, fried potatoes. But hang on! Since the world of cooking went all test tubes and lab coats, it turns out that frying potatoes is anything but simple. We shall ponder this more during the recipe.

Pimenton ahumado is smoked paprika—a spice that turns up again and again in Spanish cooking. The finest producers of smoked paprika smoke their peppers over oak fires before grinding them down into a fine powder. Aioli is similar to mayonnaise but not interchangeable. It's an obscenely garlicky emulsified sauce served with all sorts of things. Don't skip this element!

And finally the shrimp…I cook them in the shell because I think it preserves flavor that would otherwise be discarded. Personally I don't bother peeling seared shrimp and I eat the shell as well, but my daughter Ellie tells me that makes me strange. Not funny-strange or cool, mysterious strange. Just strange.

Seared shrimp with patatas bravas, chile, garlic & pimenton ahumado & aioli

SERVES 4

4 medium potatoes, cut into
   1-inch dice

6 tablespoons olive oil

16 large raw large shrimp in the shell

7 tablespoons unsalted butter

4 really ripe plum tomatoes,
   finely diced

4 garlic cloves, finely chopped

2 red chiles, finely diced

1 teaspoon sea salt

2 teaspoons smoked paprika

juice of ½ lemon

1 tablespoon chopped flat-leaf parsley

TO SERVE

1 fresh white baguette

1 quantity Aioli (see opposite)

Bring a large pan of water to a boil and add the potatoes. Bring to a simmer and cook gently, to prevent the potatoes from breaking up, until cooked through. Test one, and if you can easily crush it with a fork, they're ready. Drain the potatoes, but DON'T cool them in cold water. Allow them to steam away, in a dish, until they have cooled completely. The idea here is to rid the inside of the potato of any water, and that escaping steam is water… well, it's steam, but it was water, and would still be water trapped inside had you cooled them under running cold water!

The serious point about the cooling method is this: if you were to fry the potatoes with water still trapped inside, the water would heat up again during the frying and try to escape through the sides of the crisping potatoes, causing them to go soggy. Anyway, potato lecture over. To recap, at this point you should have steaming, cooling potatoes. When they're cold, chill them in the fridge until needed. Let's move on…

Apart from the potatoes, everything else is basically cooked to order (not counting the aioli, which needs to be made ahead of time). Heat 4 tablespoons of the oil in a frying pan. Add the cold potatoes and cook them until golden and crispy all over. Remove the potatoes out to a plate covered with paper towels to drain.

Return the pan to high heat and add the remaining oil. Lay the shrimp in the pan and cook for 2 minutes on either side. If the shrimp stick slightly, that's great and will add additional flavor! Add in the butter—it will melt and sizzle, but try to prevent it from burning. Immediately add the tomatoes. The moisture from the tomatoes will sizzle and evaporate, which is good. Continue to cook for 3 minutes.

Toss in the garlic, chiles, salt, and paprika. Sizzle for 1 minute, then return the crispy potatoes to the pan. Squeeze on the lemon juice and finish with the parsley. Toss everything together to make sure those powerful flavors mingle. Serve in bowls with crusty bread and aioli on the side.

66 There are those who put chopped garlic into mayonnaise and call it aioli—no, no, and no! Aioli is a very garlicky Spanish sauce bearing a resemblance to mayonnaise, but it should be made with olive oil and without the mayonnaise-like additions of mustard or vinegar.

Years ago I spent the summer in San Sebastian with a friend who worked at a fabulous, highly acclaimed restaurant. Being in our early twenties, we spent most evenings drinking beer and trying to pick up the beautiful local Basque girls, and by the end of each night we would be drunk but very single. We would then make our way to a late-night bar for more beer and amazingly simple but tasty, crusty baguettes filled with grilled chicken slathered in garlic aioli. Not the intended end to the evening, but very satisfying nonetheless. 99

Aioli

MAKES ENOUGH FOR 8 DECENT SERVINGS

5 garlic cloves

1 teaspoon salt

4 egg yolks

¾ cup olive oil (I use a reasonably cheap, light-tasting oil for this)

1 teaspoon smoked paprika

Bash the garlic and salt together in a mortar and pestle, then transfer to a bowl.

Add the egg yolks and whisk, then gradually whisk in the olive oil and finally the smoked paprika. Your finished aioli will be a similar consistency to store-bought mayonnaise, but bear in mind it will set up in the fridge.

66 Just say I had a lovely gastro pub close to Richmond Park in London with roaring log fires, charming waiters, a fabulous menu, an award-winning wine list and competitive prices…and just say the phone number was 020 8876 4238… you could book a table and come in and try this particular dish because it has gastro pub–type food written all over it. Just say….

There are lots of different clams found the world over. Clams are defined as bivalves, which to you and me means that they have two tightly closed shells. Have a chat with your fishmonger— they will know which edible clam types are available. Cook your clams on the day that you buy them and bear in mind that you are only getting 25 percent of the purchased weight in edible meat—the rest is shell. I usually allow half pound of raw in-the-shell clams per person for a starter and a pound for a main course. This is the sort of dish that needs to be cooked and eaten right away, so have your guests sitting while you do the cooking. 99

Clams cooked in cider with smoked bacon, chorizo, parsley & chile

SERVES 4

1 tablespoon vegetable oil

12 slices dry-cure smoked bacon, finely shredded

7oz chorizo, broken into smallish chunks

4½ lbs fresh live clams in the shell

3½ cups cider

2 red chiles, thinly sliced into rings

4 garlic cloves, finely chopped

2 shallots, thinly sliced into rings

2 tablespoons coarsely chopped flat-leaf parsley

pinch of salt

Once you have assembled all the ingredients, the cooking is fun, fast, and furious. Select a nice large pan for which you have a lid. Heat the pan over high heat until good and hot. Pour in the vegetable oil and let it get really hot. Add the bacon and chorizo and cook for 2 minutes.

Rinse the clams under cold water to remove any grit from the shells, drain and then add them to the pot—they will immediately sizzle and steam dramatically. Give the pot a good shake around in a manly fashion. Slam the lid on aggressively. Your guests will be impressed.

Now lift the lid and pour in the cider. Slam the lid back on for 2 minutes, during which time the cider will start to boil, and shake the pan a few times to mix up the clams. Lift the lid and toss in the chiles, garlic, and shallots and give everything a good stir with a wooden spoon. Keep the liquid boiling during this process.

Finally stir in the parsley and salt and immediately pour the contents of the pan into a big serving dish and stick it in the middle of the table. Serve with a lot of crusty white bread on the side.

A WORD ON COOKING CLAMS

A lot of people worry about cooking shellfish, so just to clear things up… Always store your live shellfish in the fridge. Don't put them in water—they are salt-water creatures, so tap water is the last thing they want to sit in. Just before cooking the clams, give them a rinse in cold water to remove any grit on the shells and then sift through them. At this point discard any clam that is open—an open shell means that the animal inside is dead and not safe to eat. It's always worth tapping the shell to see if it slowly shuts, because the cunning old clam might just be fooling around. Avoid eating any clams that have not opened during cooking as this again suggests that the clam may be unfit for consumption. Broadly speaking, the same applies to mussels, by the way. Right, health and safety lecture over.

Blackened chicken

SERVES 4

1 teaspoon finely ground black pepper

½ teaspoon finely ground white pepper

1 teaspoon garlic powder

1 teaspoon onion powder

1 teaspoon ground cumin

1 teaspoon cayenne pepper

½ teaspoon paprika

1 tablespoon salt

4 skinless and boneless chicken breasts

2 sticks of butter, melted

Mix all of the spices and the salt together in a bowl and set aside.

Lay the chicken breasts on a piece of parchment paper and carefully paint a layer of melted butter all over the surface of the chicken. The chicken will be cold because it's been in the fridge, so the butter will start to set quickly. Before this happens take several good pinches of the spice mix and sprinkle it on the buttered chicken, so that the chicken is completely coated in spice. Allow the butter to set for a few seconds.

Turn the chicken breasts over and do exactly the same to the other side. Be careful when maneuvering the chicken, because the set butter will become brittle. At this stage the chicken can be chilled for up to an hour.

To cook the chicken, heat a large, heavy-bottomed frying pan over high heat. Don't be tempted to add any oil. Carefully lay the chicken breasts in the pan—my pan is 12 inches in diameter and I cook 2 breasts at a time in it, but if yours is smaller, you may need to cook them separately as overcrowding the pan will result in disappointing "blackening." The pan will immediately smoke aggressively, and that's fine. Don't move the chicken—this harsh heat is important. After about 5 minutes, turn the chicken over to cook the other side. I use tongs to hold the chicken on its side so that I can blacken the edges, too. In total, the chicken breasts should take about 12 minutes to cook, but check that they are cooked through before serving—they can be finished in a hot oven if absolutely necessary.

> One of the major differences between the recipes I wrote for this book and the recipes I write in my professional life for the team in the kitchen is the tone and feel of the writing. Recipes for home cooks need to be written in a friendly, chatty, informative, arm-around-the-shoulder type way, not the "bullet point" approach I take with my chefs in the restaurant. Hollandaise, for instance:

> • Warm butter • Whisk yolks • Add reduction • Add butter • If it curdles, you're fired • Serve

> This approach would fail completely in the competitive world of cookbook publishing. My editor Sophie would certainly call me up and tell me to "pad out" my recipes with warm words of encouragement for the reader.

> My staff, on the other hand, would find it very odd if I gave them a recipe written in the home cookbook style. They wouldn't be able to deal with all the fluffy, cuddly stuff. I can hear them now: 'Seen this recipe Chef gave me? Full of long words, praise, encouragement, and warnings about hot pan handles. I like aggressive bullet points and the occasional shouting. The guy's lost it, I guess.'

> When I decided to include the following recipe in this book, I was pleased to find that I had it typed up on my computer already. I thought that it was just a quick cut-and-paste job and then on to the next recipe. But no. When I opened the document I was horrified to find that I had summarized the entire recipe in 41 words spread over 6 tiny bullet points. So I've fleshed it out, written in lots of handy hints, occasional praise, and lots of encouragement!

> This recipe is a favorite of mine at home and in the restaurant, and it's perfect for a dinner party—simple to make, packed with flavor and you can prepare it in advance. Of course you don't have to wait until you are entertaining friends—feel free to eat it on a Wednesday night in front of the TV.

Smoked paprika chicken casserole with chickpeas, peppers & chorizo

SERVES 4

A QUICK WORD ABOUT THE INGREDIENTS

Not all chorizo sausage is created equal. As with so much in life, you get what you pay for. I use an Alejandro chorizo, which I buy from a specialist Spanish supplier, but some supermarkets stock a variety of chorizos. Look out for a rustic cooking chorizo made of pork, paprika, garlic, seasoning, and nothing else. This recipe also calls for chickpeas. If you can be bothered to soak and cook dried chickpeas, your casserole will be even better. I do at work; I don't at home.

CONTINUED OVERLEAF... ——————▶

Smoked paprika chicken casserole with chickpeas, peppers & chorizo

CONTINUED FROM PAGE 83

3 tablespoons olive oil

1 large red onion, thinly sliced

large sprig of thyme

2 garlic cloves, thinly sliced

1 teaspoon fennel seeds

good pinch of red pepper flakes

generous pinch of saffron

1 teaspoon smoked paprika

1 lb chorizo, diced

2 red peppers, thinly sliced

2 yellow peppers thinly sliced

3 plum tomatoes, cut into 8 wedges

1 tablespoon vegetable oil

2 chicken breasts, halved

4 chicken thighs

14oz can chickpeas, rinsed and drained (or equivalent soaked and cooked dried chickpeas)

sugar, to taste (optional, depending on how ripe your tomatoes are)

salt and freshly ground black pepper

Heat half of the olive oil in a large, heavy-bottomed, lidded pot. Add the onion, thyme, and garlic and let everything sizzle in the hot oil for about 3 minutes or until softened but not colored. Add the fennel seeds, red pepper flakes, saffron and smoked paprika and stir.

Add the remaining olive oil and, when it has heated up a little, add the chorizo, peppers, and tomato wedges. Sizzle for 5 minutes. Pour in half a mug of cold water, pop the lid on, reduce the heat to low, and leave everything to stew gently for about 15 minutes.

Meanwhile, heat a large frying pan over high heat, add the vegetable oil, and cook the chicken, in batches if necessary, until sealed (when a chef asks you to seal something, all they want you to do is brown the outside rather than cooking it through). Set aside.

Back to the pot. When you lift the lid you should find that the vegetables have all softened and the chorizo is cooked. If not, cook for a few minutes more. Tip in the chickpeas and stir, then add the chicken, pushing it into the stew. Put the lid back on and again leave to stew away for another 15 minutes or until the chicken is cooked through.

You are basically done, but have a taste. You may think it should be slightly sweeter, in which case add a pinch or two of sugar. I expect it will need a pinch of salt and a twist of pepper, too.

The options for serving this are varied. You could do some mashed or new potatoes, but as the chickpeas are quite filling you may not need anything too heavy. I think the best additions are a slice of ciabatta fried in olive oil and a dollop of Aioli (see page 77).

One of my favorite local Indian restaurants has this dish on the menu. The last time I was there I asked for the recipe. The waiter went off to the kitchen, returning with more of a shopping list than a recipe, so I've played around a bit and I think I've got close!

This dish originates from Goa, a state in the southwest of India. The local cuisine is now world-famous due in no small part to the fact that Goa has a thriving tourist industry. Two particular flavors come up time and again: the sour, piquant flavor achieved through the use of vinegar, wine, or tamarind, and the fiery heat of chiles and spice—both of which are present here. As with many curries, this dish really does benefit from being cooked a day in advance if you can bear holding out.

Murgh moelho

SERVES 4

2 tablespoons vegetable oil

12 chicken thighs

4 teaspoons cumin seeds

3 teaspoons yellow mustard seeds

good pinch of red pepper flakes

1 teaspoon ground turmeric

2 teaspoons chile powder

5 tablespoons white wine vinegar

2 onions, halved and thinly sliced

7 garlic cloves, crushed

1 cup water

1 teaspoon salt

Heat a large frying pan over high heat, add 1 tablespoon vegetable oil and cook the chicken thighs until they have a good roasty color all over (you're not trying to cook them at this stage, so just cook until browned). The next job is a strange one. You need to select a knife with a nice sharp tip and prick the chicken thighs all over, making at least 15 small incisions in each thigh. Don't skip this step because it helps the penetration of flavor as the chicken cooks. Set the chicken thighs aside.

Meanwhile, heat a small frying pan and dry-fry the cumin seeds, mustard seeds, and red pepper flakes until they release a strong aroma and start to brown very slightly. They may also pop as they heat up. Leave to cool, grind to a fine powder in a mortar and pestle, then mix in the turmeric and chile powder. Pour the vinegar into a large bowl and stir in the spice mix.

Place the chicken thighs in the bowl with the vinegar and spice mix and give them a good stir, making sure the vinegar and spice are rubbed all over the chicken pieces. Leave this to one side for 20 minutes.

Heat a pan with a tight-fitting lid over medium-high heat and add the remaining vegetable oil. Add the onions and garlic and cook for 15 minutes or until they are a really dark brown. Add the chicken thighs, scraping in any spicy vinegar residue from the bowl. Pour in the water, add the salt, and bring to a simmer. Reduce the heat to low, cover, and cook for 45 minutes or until the chicken is tender and cooked through, the kitchen smells amazing, and you are very hungry indeed. Resist! Transfer the curry to an ovenproof dish and leave to cool, then cover and refrigerate overnight.

When you are ready to eat, simply preheat the oven to 325°F and put the dish in the oven for 25–30 minutes to reheat the curry. Serve with white Basmati rice.

> When I was kid I can recall my dad singing songs in the car as we drove around the countryside. This in itself is bad enough (I know, because my own children have complained when I've struck up a tune), but what made it much worse was that he only knew three songs that could even vaguely be described as contemporary popular music. One of these had been a big hit a few years before (quite a few years before!) for Fats Domino and was entitled 'Jambalaya (On the Bayou)'. The original version of this song is by Hank Williams and very much celebrates all things Cajun, particularly the cuisine. 'Jambalaya and a crawfish pie and filé gumbo' is how the chorus starts and, frankly, we could accuse Hank of simply putting a tune to any number of local Cajun-Creole restaurant menus, but the bottom line is, he's provided me with a very nifty recipe intro and I'm grateful for that.
>
> Jambalaya is a rice dish made with peppers, onions, celery, chicken, sausage, and seafood and, once cooked, it is often baked in the oven. I've only had Jambalaya once but really enjoyed it. Crawfish pie is exactly what it says (crawfish is like a lobster), leaving only filé gumbo requiring an explanation. Gumbo is a stew, which has a base of onions, celery, and peppers (known locally as the Holy Trinity) and can contain meat or fish. Okra, hot sausage, and spice are the other familiar characteristics.
>
> The word filé that Mr Williams uses in his song refers to the dried and ground leaves of the sassafras tree found in North America. This spice is also a useful thickening agent.
>
> While gumbo has a very eclectic family tree—West African, Spanish, and French—it is the official dish of the state of Louisiana and the main man in those parts is chef Paul Prudhomme. I was given his book many years ago and in it are various gumbo recipes, from catfish to squirrel and everything in between. The following recipe is my version of gumbo based on attempts at several of his! The dish is a labor of love, so make it when you are assured of an audience who will appreciate and applaud your efforts.
>
> Oh, and by the way, the other two songs my dad used to sing were 'Yellow Submarine' by The Beatles and 'Chirpy Chirpy Cheep Cheep' by Middle of the Road... I had a tough childhood!

Chicken gumbo
(son of a gun, we'll have big fun on the bayou)

SERVES 8 GENEROUSLY

FOR STAGE 1

2 large chickens, about 4 lbs each

6 garlic cloves, crushed to a purée with a little coarse salt

1 tablespoon cayenne pepper

1 tablespoon ground black pepper

This recipe works best if broken down into stages.

Stage 1 is preparing and marinating the chicken. The day before you want to serve the dish, cut each whole chicken into six by dividing the drumsticks, thighs, and breasts. Remove the skin from all the pieces and cut the breasts in half. To make the marinade, mix the garlic with the cayenne pepper and black pepper to form a paste. Set a quarter of the paste aside and rub the remainder all over the chicken pieces, rubbing really well, then chill for up to 24 hours.

MORE INGREDIENTS OVERLEAF ...

CONTINUED... ——————▶

Chicken gumbo (son of a gun, we'll have big fun on the bayou)

CONTINUED FROM PAGE 87

FOR STAGE 2

2½ cups chicken stock

3 tablespoons butter

3 tablespoons all-purpose flour

14oz can chopped tomatoes

FOR STAGE 3

vegetable oil, for frying

1 onion, diced

1 green pepper, diced

4 celery sticks, sliced

2 good pinches of salt

3 teaspoons filé powder (found on the internet or specialist spice shops)

6 kabanos sausages, about 5oz, cut into thickish slices (chorizo or similar cured sausage would work, too)

2oz ham, diced

2 hard-boiled eggs, chopped

8 scallions, sliced

7oz okra, cut into thin slices

2 tablespoons chopped parsley

Stage 2 is the actual cooking bit and for this we need to make a simple version of a velouté sauce (to you and me that means a chicken sauce thickened with butter and flour). Pour the chicken stock into a large pan or pot, cover and bring to a simmer. Rub the butter and flour together to form a paste. Drop small pellets of the flour and butter paste into the simmering chicken stock and whisk so that it breaks up and disperses. After a few minutes you should have a fairly smooth sauce with the consistency of heavy cream. Add the tomatoes and simmer for another 10 minutes.

Meanwhile, heat a nonstick frying pan and add the marinated chicken pieces. Cook until they take on a golden-brown color (they will still be raw inside at this point). Drop the sealed chicken into the sauce and simmer for 20 minutes or until the chicken is just cooked—it will continue to cook during stage 3, so don't allow it to overcook now.

Stage 3 is finishing off. Bear in mind that when this part is done you'll need friends present, rice cooked, and some zydeco music on the stereo. Heat a little vegetable oil in a small pan and gently cook the onion, green pepper, and celery for 2–3 minutes until softened but not colored. Transfer the vegetables to the chicken pot. Stir in the reserved marinade and add the salt and filé powder—this will very slightly thicken the sauce. Finally stir in the remaining ingredients until heated through and serve.

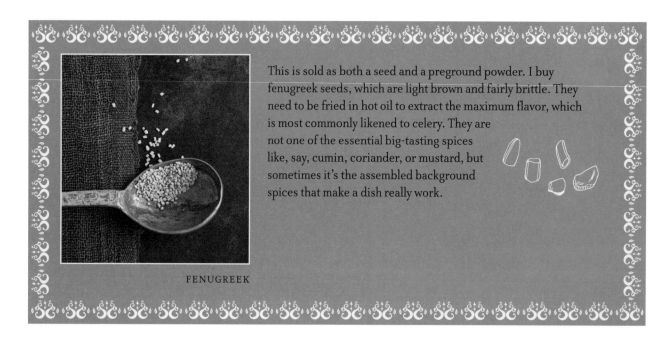

FENUGREEK

This is sold as both a seed and a preground powder. I buy fenugreek seeds, which are light brown and fairly brittle. They need to be fried in hot oil to extract the maximum flavor, which is most commonly likened to celery. They are not one of the essential big-tasting spices like, say, cumin, coriander, or mustard, but sometimes it's the assembled background spices that make a dish really work.

My restaurant, The Victoria, recently hosted a special dinner involving several very talented chefs each cooking a course using higher-welfare pork. I was eager to serve something that was in the style of our usual menu, and this is the dish that we created for that evening.

Our version for the evening was cooked *à la sous-vide* in a water bath. For those of you who don't practice high-end molecular gastronomy (count me among you), a water bath cooks proteins enclosed in a vacuum bag at a very low temperature for a very long time, thus reducing spoilage and other changes that occur when cooking food conventionally. Water baths are very expensive and I'm not about to suggest you invest in one for this recipe. Frankly, we didn't ever use ours enough at the restaurant, so I took it home where my wife now uses it as a foot bath!

The dish itself has mixed parentage, so to speak. The spice mix used is very Sri Lankan in flavor and method, yet later on in the dish a Thai influence comes to bear. When you cast your eyes down the list of ingredients, you may feel a little wary of trying this, but I've tried to point out little tips that could make the job easier. A quick heads-up on a couple of ingredients that may seem unfamiliar—kaffir lime leaves are used in many Asian cuisines and they have a wonderful flavor and aroma, and galangal is a member of the ginger family (it looks like a spiky version of ginger) that, when eaten raw, has a more pungent flavor. You should find both of these ingredients in larger supermarkets but also in any good Asian store.

Pork cheeks are boneless nuggets of meat that need a long, slow cooking, ideal for this sort of curry. I've never seen them in a supermarket, but I have managed to buy them from my butcher. It's worth ordering them a couple of days in advance because he may well not keep them in stock. A large dice of boneless shoulder meat would be a good second option. The Soured Mango "Noodles" are not essential, but they do give the finished dish a lovely fresh flavor.

Braised pork cheeks with coconut & lime leaf served with soured mango "noodles"

SERVES 4

FOR THE SRI LANKAN-STYLE CURRY POWDER

1 tablespoon uncooked Basmati rice

3 tablespoons coriander seeds

2 tablespoons cumin seeds

2 tablespoons fennel seeds

3-inch cinnamon stick

10 green cardamom pods

½ teaspoon black mustard seeds

1½ teaspoons fenugreek seeds

1 teaspoon black peppercorns

3 dried chiles

First make the Sri Lankan-style curry powder. This can be done a few days ahead of the braised pork cheeks, and the quantities given here will provide more than you need, so store what's left in an old spice jar. Heat a frying pan but don't add any oil. Tip in the rice and toast until browned, but don't let it over-color or it will blacken. Transfer the rice to a plate and set aside to cool. Now do exactly the same with the spices: tip them all into the pan together and dry-roast them until they start to darken slightly. Transfer the spices to the plate with the rice and allow to cool. Mix the rice and the spices together and grind them to a powder in either an electric spice grinder or using a mortar and pestle.

MORE INGREDIENTS OVERLEAF …

CONTINUED OVERLEAF ⟶

Braised pork cheeks with coconut & lime leaf served with soured mango "noodles"

CONTINUED FROM PAGE 89

vegetable oil, for cooking

12 pork cheeks, trimmed of all fat
and sinew

1 onion, finely sliced

2 garlic cloves, finely chopped

2-inch piece of fresh galangal,
peeled and roughly chopped

1 lemongrass stalk, roughly chopped

3 small hot green chiles,
sliced into rings

6 kaffir lime leaves

10 curry leaves

½ teaspoon ground turmeric

½ teaspoon chile powder

3⅓ cups coconut milk

1 cup water

juice of 1–2 limes, to taste

2–3 tablespoons liquid palm sugar,
to taste

up to 2 tablespoons fish sauce, to taste

Soured Mango "Noodles" (see
page 184), and sticky rice, to serve

To make the braised pork cheeks, heat a large pot and pour in a little vegetable oil. Place the pork cheeks into the hot pan and sear until well colored on all sides. Remove from the pan and set aside. Don't wash out the pan; just add a little more vegetable oil and carry on cooking.

Toss in the onion, garlic, galangal, lemongrass, and chiles into the pan. Allow everything to slowly sizzle away and caramelize slightly. This should take 10–15 minutes. Add the lime leaves, curry leaves, 2½ teaspoons Sri Lankan-style curry powder, the turmeric, and chile powder and stir. Pour in the coconut milk and the water and return the pork cheeks to the pan. Slowly bring the sauce up to a simmer and cook slowly for 1½ hours.

Fish out a pork cheek and put it on a plate. If the meat is tender enough to cut easily with a spoon, the cheeks are ready. If not, return to the pan and continue to cook for a few minutes longer. Once the cheeks are cooked, remove them all from the sauce and set aside.

Increase the temperature to high and bring the sauce to a boil. Continue to cook until the sauce has reduced a little, then pour through a sieve to remove all the bits. Return the pork cheeks to the sauce and either cool down and refrigerate until required or finish the sauce and serve up.

When you are ready to serve, stir in the lime juice, palm sugar and fish sauce until you feel the taste is just right. Serve each person 3 pork cheeks and pour on some sauce. Place a pile of Soured Mango Noodles on top of the pork cheeks and serve with plain boiled sticky rice.

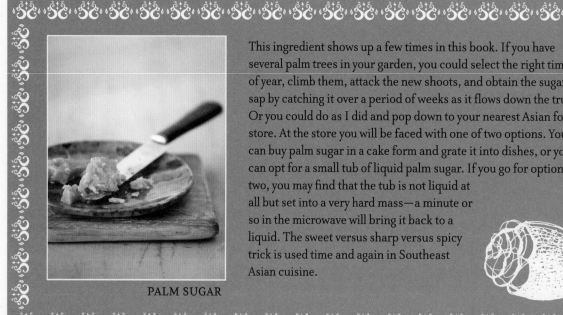

This ingredient shows up a few times in this book. If you have several palm trees in your garden, you could select the right time of year, climb them, attack the new shoots, and obtain the sugary sap by catching it over a period of weeks as it flows down the trunk. Or you could do as I did and pop down to your nearest Asian food store. At the store you will be faced with one of two options. You can buy palm sugar in a cake form and grate it into dishes, or you can opt for a small tub of liquid palm sugar. If you go for option two, you may find that the tub is not liquid at all but set into a very hard mass—a minute or so in the microwave will bring it back to a liquid. The sweet versus sharp versus spicy trick is used time and again in Southeast Asian cuisine.

PALM SUGAR

HOW TO SPATCHCOCK & MARINATE THE QUAIL

"Spatchcock" (an excellent culinary word) describes a butchering technique, which is used to prepare a bird such as a chicken, or indeed a quail, for grilling over coals or in a grill pan. The backbone is removed so that the bird can be flattened out—thus it's easier to cook. If you buy your meat from a decent butcher, he or she will almost definitely be able to do this for you, but in case they're shut for the day and you have to go to the supermarket, here is what you do. A quail has the same anatomy as a chicken only smaller, so hopefully you'll understand the basic shape and make-up.

Place the bird on a cutting board with the legs pointing toward you. Open up the cavity and you will see the backbone lying flat on the board, running through the middle of the cavity. Poke a sharp knife inside the bird all the way to the other end. Keep the knife blade to one side of the backbone and cut down along the bone. Repeat this maneuver on the other side of the backbone, which should release it completely. Give the bird a push down with the palm of your hand and it should remain flat. You have just spatchcocked your first quail! Put your flattened birds in the fridge while you prepare the marinade.

For the marinade, squeeze the orange juice into a bowl and add the olive oil, sumac, thyme leaves, honey, and ground cumin. Stir everything up. Take the spatchcocked quail and rub them all over with the marinade. Place in a dish, pour on any remaining marinade, and leave in the fridge for a couple of hours—overnight would be fine, too.

Whoever first discovered that quails were good to eat was definitely one very hungry person. A quail is a tiny bird with all its feathers—it's even smaller when you get its feathers off. Anyway, that intrepid cook was right: they are tasty little things. The meat is very similar to chicken or guinea fowl and well worth trying if you haven't already.

The celeriac slaw is a bit of an old favorite, turning up from time to time at the restaurant with a variety of dishes. If you are new to the joys of celeriac, imagine a vegetable that looks like a large turnip with a similar density and texture but with a sweet, subtle, celery flavor. It is a great partner to the crisp red apple and creamy mayonnaise. The pomegranate dressing not only looks spectacular but also works very well with both the charred meat of the quail and the richness of the slaw. 99

Chargrilled quail with sumac, celeriac & apple slaw & pomegranate dressing

SERVES 4

4 quail, spatchcocked (see left)

juice of 1 orange

½ cup olive oil for the marinade, plus a little extra for grilling the quail

2 teaspoons sumac

½ teaspoon thyme leaves

¼ cup honey

2 teaspoons ground cumin

FOR THE CELERIAC & APPLE SLAW

6oz chunk of celeriac, finely sliced and then finely shredded into long, thin matchsticks

2 red apples

½ tablespoon grainy mustard

½ tablespoon honey

4–5 tablespoons mayonnaise (yes, a shop-bought one is fine!)

FOR THE POMEGRANATE DRESSING

1 pomegranate

2 tablespoons sugar

¼ cup olive oil

Spatchcock and marinate the quail—see left. When the time comes to cook the quail, take them out of the fridge and give them a final rub with the marinade before laying, skin-side down on your barbecue or hot grill pan. Because they are coated with spice and honey, the birds will catch and char, but that's good; the burnt skin will add an important flavor to the dish. Give them 4 minutes on the skin side, then flip over and cook on the "B" side. They may buckle slightly, but just push them down flat again using your tongs. In total your quail will need about 12 minutes.

MAKING THE CELERIAC & APPLE SLAW

Bring a pot of water to a boil and toss in your very finely shredded celeriac. Give it 1 minute in the boiling water and then pour it into a colander. Tip the hot blanched celeriac into a bowl of cold water to stop the cooking process. Once it's cold, tip it back into the colander and allow it to drain. I sometimes pat it with a clean cloth to make sure all the excess water is removed. Place the drained celeriac into a mixing bowl.

Take the red apples and slice them finely as far as the core. Lay the slices on a cutting board and cut into fine matchsticks. Add this to the celeriac. Mix the grainy mustard, honey, and mayonnaise and pour this over the celeriac and apple. Mix everything up and keep chilled in the fridge until needed.

THE POMEGRANATE DRESSING

The dressing can be done ahead of time if you are the well-organized type! Cut the pomegranate in half and, after marveling at how beautiful it is inside, scrape out all the fleshy seeds and transfer them to a bowl. Squeeze, press, and mash the pomegranate to release as much juice as possible. From 1 pomegranate I got about ½ cup of juice. Place the juice in a small pan and simmer for 5 minutes with the sugar. Remove, cool to room temperature, and then whisk in the olive oil. This should result in a rich-red, tangy dressing to trickle over and around the quail with the slaw on the side.

> This dish has its roots in Richmond, West London... sort of. It's an irony, but the food most restaurant staff eat is pretty ordinary. I've never worked anywhere where the chefs actually sit down to eat; food is always eaten on the go, while running around setting up for either lunch or dinner. French fries, omelettes, baked beans, and salads feature heavily.
>
> Curry is without a doubt a favorite with the kitchen staff. We can "curry up" just about anything. On one joyous occasion, our butcher sent us an extra leg of lamb by mistake. The right and proper course of action would have been to call him and send it back, but where's the fun in that? Instead it was decided that this 'free' gift should be 'curried up' for the boys.
>
> After a bit of research, a suitable recipe was found and we set about making this Kashmiri-style curry. We have made it countless times since, each time tweaking the original recipe slightly until we have the perfect curry. This is that very curry, but you don't need six sweaty chefs to make or eat it. We'll come over by all means, but it's so good that you can safely feed it to your friends, and we have also put it on the menu a few times since.
>
> Kashmir is in northwestern India and can lay claim to many fine culinary inventions, including this one. Our version isn't hot and fiery but is made up of layers of flavor through the use of various aromatic spices. I'd like to thank our butcher for his part in developing this dish.

"Rista" meatballs with saffron & rose water

SERVES 4

2¼ lbs boneless lamb, preferably from the leg, diced

1½ tablespoons coriander seeds

1 teaspoon yellow mustard seeds

1 teaspoon cumin seeds

1 teaspoon fenugreek seeds

1½ teaspoons chile powder

4 garlic cloves, crushed to a paste

¼ cup gram (chickpea) flour

½ teaspoon salt

vegetable oil, for frying

To make the meatballs, the first job is to grind the meat to a fine paste— I know that doesn't sound appealing, but it will be in the end! This is best done in a food processor. Do the grinding in manageable amounts, then put the ground lamb in a bowl in the fridge until needed.

Heat a frying pan and dry-fry the coriander, mustard, cumin, and fenugreek seeds until they start to brown very slightly. Leave to cool, then grind to a fine powder in a mortar and pestle.

Take the lamb out of the fridge and add the freshly ground spice mixture along with the chile powder, garlic, gram flour, and salt. Mix well to combine and then roll the seasoned meat into balls about the size of a golf ball using your hands. The mixture should make about 16 meatballs. Heat a frying pan and add a little vegetable oil. Cook the meatballs in batches until they are a rich brown color all over and then pop them onto a plate to one side (they shouldn't be cooked through at this stage).

Now find a pot to cook the curry sauce. Heat it over medium heat and add a little vegetable oil. Add the onions, garlic, and ginger and cook for 20 minutes or more over medium heat until they are a dark brown color. Don't rush this stage or the ingredients will burn—remember, dark brown, not black! If they stick on the bottom or the sides of the pan, add a tablespoon of water and stir vigorously to work the stuck bits back in to the bulk. This caramelization adds an important element to the finished flavor.

vegetable oil, for frying

2 onions, finely chopped

5 garlic cloves, finely chopped

¾ cup fresh peeled and grated ginger

½ cup plain yogurt

5 cloves

4 cardamom pods

5-inch cinnamon stick, broken into 3

4 teaspoons red pepper flakes

1 teaspoon asafoetida

1 teaspoon ground ginger

7 cups water

½ cup dried green lentils

½ teaspoon salt

good pinch of saffron

3 teaspoons rose water

Add the yogurt, cloves, cardamom, cinnamon, red pepper flakes, asafoetida, and ground ginger. Continue to cook until the yogurt is completely reduced and almost dry. Pour in the water and add the lentils. Bring to a simmer and cook for another 10 minutes.

Add the colored meatballs and the salt. Reduce the heat and cook slowly for 40 minutes or until the meatballs are cooked through and the lentils are soft and breaking up slightly. Remove the meatballs from the sauce and set aside. Blend the sauce very roughly using an immersion blender to allow the lentils to thicken it slightly, but don't overdo it as the sauce should have plenty of texture. Return the meatballs to the pan and stir in the saffron and rose water just before serving. Kashmir is a traditional rice-growing region, so a bowl of Basmati is the very best thing to serve with this.

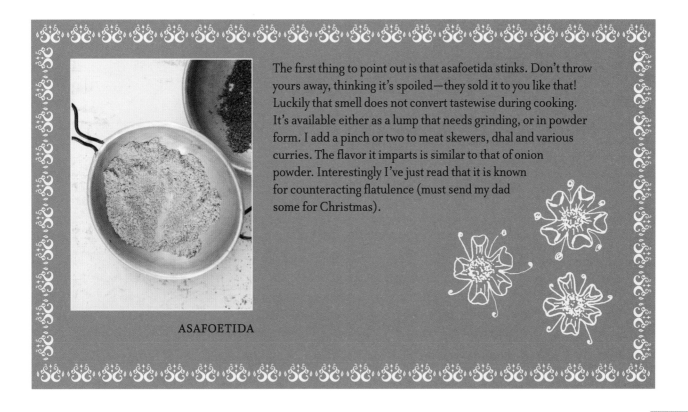

The first thing to point out is that asafoetida stinks. Don't throw yours away, thinking it's spoiled—they sold it to you like that! Luckily that smell does not convert tastewise during cooking. It's available either as a lump that needs grinding, or in powder form. I add a pinch or two to meat skewers, dhal and various curries. The flavor it imparts is similar to that of onion powder. Interestingly I've just read that it is known for counteracting flatulence (must send my dad some for Christmas).

ASAFOETIDA

" This is an old favorite both at home and at the restaurant. I've suggested using lamb rump because it's one of my preferred cuts, but you could use a rack of lamb, loin, or even a shoulder. The salsa is really simple and can be made in advance and served at room temperature, and the baba ghanoush is also best made well before required, so all in all, the work involved just before serving is minimal, making this a great dinner-party dish. Dhana jeera can be bought in specialist spice shops, but don't bother since you can easily make your own by roasting and grinding cumin and coriander seeds. This dish is really an assembly of small elements, so I've divided the recipe up into stages with suggestions on when to cook what. "

Dhana jeera spiced lamb with sweet potato, baba ghanoush & eggplant salsa

SERVES 4

3 tablespoons coriander seeds

2 tablespoons cumin seeds

½ cup olive oil

4 thick-cut lamb chops, each about
    6oz (ask your butcher and they
    will know what you want!)

vegetable oil, for frying

1 quantity Baba Ghanoush
    (see page 182), to serve

FOR THE EGGPLANT SALSA

1½ cups olive oil

1 eggplant, cut into ½-inch dice

4 garlic cloves, crushed to a paste

1 cup shredded cilantro

grated zest and juice of 1 lime

4 red chiles, finely chopped

FOR THE SWEET POTATOES

4 sweet potatoes, peeled and
    cut into 1-inch dice

olive oil, for frying

pinch of salt (optional)

MAKING THE DHANA JEERA AND MARINATING THE LAMB

This job is best done the day before you intend to eat the dish. Dry-fry the coriander and cumin seeds in a hot frying pan until they start to change color. They will smoke a bit and smell fantastic. Set the seeds aside to cool, then grind them to as fine a powder as you can using a spice grinder or a mortar and pestle. You will need 4 teaspoons of dhana jeera for this recipe and the remainder can be stored in an old spice jar.

To marinate the lamb, whisk together 4 teaspoons of the dhana jeera with the olive oil in a bowl to form a paste. Place the lamb in the bowl and rub thoroughly with the spice paste. Chill in the fridge until required.

MAKING THE SALSA

Make the salsa up to 2 hours before serving. Heat a wok and pour in the olive oil. When the oil is nice and hot, add the eggplant and stir-fry it until it turns a light golden-brown color. Transfer the eggplant to a colander placed over a bowl to catch the oil. Set the oil aside and allow to cool completely.

Put the eggplant into another bowl and add the garlic, cilantro, lime zest and juice, and chiles. When the oil is cool, pour it into the bowl containing the eggplant and stir everything up well. Leave to stand at room temperature.

PREPARING THE SWEET POTATOES

Boil the sweet potatoes in a pan of water until just tender. Drain and leave to cool, then chill until required (this could be done up to a day in advance).

TURNING ALL OF THAT INTO THE DISH ITSELF!

Your friends have arrived, they are drinking your best wine and they are building up an appetite, so...

Preheat the oven to 350°F. Heat a small frying pan over medium heat and add a little vegetable oil.

Cook the spiced lamb in the pan until roasty brown all over. Transfer them to the oven and cook for about 12 minutes until cooked to medium.

Heat a good splash of olive oil in a separate, larger frying pan and add the sweet potatoes. Cook until browned all over and beginning to caramelize—this gives them a fabulous taste. Add a pinch of salt, if liked.

Place a pile of potatoes into each person's bowl, halve each lamb chop (if needed) and pop that on top of the sweet potato. Spoon on some eggplant salsa and dollop on some Baba Ghanoush.

Done!

My business partner Greg gave me a barbecue for my birthday last year. He's a Kiwi, which means he is genetically programmed to barbecue at a moment's notice. I, on the other hand, have never been overly crazy about barbecues. For me the kitchen offers so much more scope and control when cooking, and I'd always noted that whenever I was invited to a friend's barbecue the cooking would be done by the partner who was normally only allowed to pour and serve drinks at a regular dinner party (among my friends that normally means the male half of the team). Men like to cook, but only if there is a suitably adoring audience. They don't go for the mundane budget-controlled cooking that takes place from Monday to Thursday, but give them a barbecue and a crowd, and all of a sudden they're experts at cooking everything from pork chops to shrimp. Or so they think.

I believe one of the big mistakes when having a barbecue is the tendency to feel that you must cook such a wide range of meats—this inevitably means that everyone eats their meal in tiny stages as the next wave of chops, sausages, or skewers comes off the hot coals. My advice is to pick one decent cut of meat and cook it beautifully. Here is one such meat. A whole leg of lamb is perfect for the grill because the outside will benefit from the high heat and flames while the center of the meat stays pink and sweet. I would suggest (and not merely for self-marketing purposes) that you serve this with Roasted Vegetable Couscous (see page 108) and a bowl of Tzatziki (see page 182).

BUTTERFLYING A LEG OF LAMB

I suggest seeking your butcher's assistance with the lamb. Ask him or her to remove the bone completely and to cut open the leg so that it becomes a large, boneless, flat piece of meat. This style of preparation is called "butterflying" and the resulting piece of lamb will cook relatively quickly, and will also be very easy to carve.

Barbecued marinated leg of lamb

A DECENT-SIZED LEG SHOULD EASILY FEED 6—8 HUNGRY FRIENDS

1 leg of lamb, about 5½ lbs on the
    bone or 3 lbs boned, boned and
    butterflied (explanation opposite!)

FOR THE MARINADE

1 glass red wine

4 star anise

2 cinnamon sticks

4 cloves

1 tablespoon coriander seeds

1 cup medium sherry

1 orange, cut into 8 thick slices

2 heads of garlic, quartered

sprig of rosemary

1 tablespoon sugar

½ cup olive oil

The marinade needs to hit the lamb at least 24 hours prior to lift-off, so the day before your barbecue pour the wine into a small pan and bring to a simmer. Toss in the star anise, cinnamon, cloves, and coriander seeds (the heat of the wine will bring out the flavors of the spices a little more than if you just make a raw, cold marinade). Simmer for a minute or two, then remove from the heat and set aside to cool completely.

Pour the wine and spices into a bowl and add the sherry, orange slices, garlic, rosemary, sugar, and oil. This is the marinade ready to go. Lay the lamb in a large baking dish and pour on the marinade. It should cover the lamb but if it doesn't quite, you may need to turn the meat over occasionally. Leave to marinate in the fridge for 24 hours.

About an hour before cooking the lamb, remove it from the marinade and pick off any of the bits that may have stuck to the meat. Preheat the barbecue and place the lamb over very hot coals (about 4 inches from the surface of the coals). Let it sizzle away undisturbed for 5—6 minutes so that it really starts to color. Turn it over and do the same on the other side, then, if your barbecue allows, lift the rack to increase the distance between coals and meat to about 8 inches. This will reduce the risk of burning the meat. The total cooking time will very much depend on the size of the leg, but should be around 45 minutes—I would turn it over at least twice more during this time. If you are lucky enough to own a food thermometer, take your lamb off the barbecue when the core temperature reaches 130—140°F.

A large chunk of meat like this should ideally be allowed to rest before being carved and eaten. That way the muscle relaxes, meaning the juices are kept within the meat rather than pouring out all over the cutting board, or worse, your best friend's wife's lap.

Apparently the UK's Guild of Food Writers has nearly 400 authors, journalists, and columnists on its books. I'm not one of them. I had half hoped that one day I would get the old tap-on-the-shoulder and be taken off to an oak-paneled room, deep below a private members' club, where I would be secretly inducted into this society after undergoing various exotic (culinary-based) rituals. Well, not any more. I am about to deliver my ambitions a fatal blow... I am listing among the ingredients for this dish a 'meat curry prepared meal'(!). It's a shameful ingredient but one I can justify, even if it does mean that I will never again be commissioned to write a cookbook.

This is one of my favorite dishes in the world. It's a simple mix of fresh ingredients, stir-fried with chopped bread, meat curry, and egg. Kottu roti is a very popular dish in Sri Lanka, often sold as street food. As well as the amazing aroma and the incredible taste, it's also the *sound* of kottu roti that is so memorable. The dish is traditionally cooked on a flat hotplate or griddle and the ingredients are maneuvered and chopped with large blades similar to those used by a baker to cut dough. The guys have a blade in either hand and they chop, chop, chop the ingredients as they are cooking. Each vendor appears to have a slightly different rhythm and style and the sound is hypnotic. If you type "kottu roti" into a search engine, you'll see videos of these guys at work. Gil Scott-Heron would have given anything for a percussionist with their flare!

The actual cooking of kottu roti is relatively simple but the problem is that the list of ingredients in most recipes includes items that need cooking before they can be listed as ingredients, if you see what I mean. The roti bread used is called *gothamba* and most recipes seem to assume that you will have a pile of this stuff lying around! And then halfway through, they order you to add your cold meat curry, which is a complete recipe in itself. My aim is to try to find a quicker, simpler way of getting you to give this dish a go. Therefore, at the risk of jeopardizing my career, I'm suggesting that you purchase a different yet useable bread for this dish and that you either use up a leftover meat curry or simply buy a prepared one. If this works and you love it, then please look up a genuine kottu recipe, make your own gothamba roti, buy the blades and griddle plate, and get chopping for real.

Meat kottu roti

SERVES 4

CURRY NOTE

You can use any type of meat curry here. The Basic Curry (see page 126) could be made specifically for this dish or (better still) use leftover curry, or buy a prepared curry, but in all cases bear in mind the weight given here is for the meat only and you should remove the meat from any gravy or sauce before using.

CONTINUED... ⟶

Meat kottu roti

CONTINUED FROM PAGE 100

2 tablespoons vegetable oil

1 large onion, chopped

3 garlic cloves, chopped

⅓ cup peeled and grated ginger

50 curry leaves

2 green bird's eye chiles, finely sliced

4 scallions, shredded

2 medium carrots, grated

1½ teaspoons cumin seeds

1½ teaspoons black mustard seeds

1 teaspoon salt

6 roti or paratha cut into small strips

1 lb prepared meat curry
   (see Curry Note on page 100)

4 eggs, beaten

shredded iceberg lettuce, to garnish

I don't have a griddle plate at home, so I use a wok to make kottu roti, and I shall assume that you too are more likely to have a wok than a full-on griddle set up in your kitchen. You will also need a large metal kitchen spoon to use for chopping and stir-frying. The following cooking process will take about 8 minutes in total. Fast food!

Heat a wok on the largest burner. We need to have a good high heat throughout this process. Pour in 1 tablespoon of the vegetable oil and get it really hot. Cook the onion, garlic, ginger, curry leaves, chiles, scallions, and carrots—use your spoon to move everything around in the wok. A little color is a good thing at this point. Stir in the cumin and mustard seeds and the salt. Add the remaining oil and toss in the strips of bread along with the meat curry.

Chop and stir, ensuring that everything comes into contact with the hot wok in order to heat through properly. Continue to chop and stir and try to find your natural rhythm—we are talking upbeat and funky, not a mournful ballad! Pour in the eggs and chop and stir these through as well. As they cook, the eggs will give a springy texture to the dish.

It's ready! Portion into bowls, sprinkle over the lettuce and serve.

CURRY LEAF

This is one of my favorite ingredients, but first things first. Curry leaf is not what is used to make curry powder. Yes, it is used in curries, but that's different. Curry leaf comes from a small tree. The leaves are sold in clusters attached to a main stem. They can be dried or frozen but are always better fresh. You can scrunch them up and add them to your cooking, but the best extraction of flavor is through cooking them. I have seen the use of curry leaf in Asian cuisine likened to that of bay leaf in European cuisine, but I feel that's doing it an injustice. I've regularly tossed bay leaves into stews and sauces and wondered if they make any real difference at all, but curry leaf has an incredible flavor that's instantly recognizable.

ALLSPICE, PUMPKIN PIE SPICE &
CHINESE FIVE-SPICE

This small section is concerned with three distinct spices. However, they are not that distinct because people seem to confuse one with another very easily. Allspice is a single berry mainly grown in Jamaica. Apparently it got its name because it resembles cloves and pepper in flavor. I grind the dried berries and use them in pickles and marinades.

Pumpkin pie spice is an assortment of sweet spices, by which I mean spices often associated with sweeter flavors, so cinnamon, nutmeg, and cloves are nearly always present, and my jar also contains cassia and ginger. I associate pumpkin pie spice with desserts such as apple pie, apple crumble, fruitcakes, and, of course, pumpkin pie.

Chinese five-spice, on the other hand, has more savory connotations. Generally it's available as a ground powder made up of fennel seed, cassia, star anise, sichuan pepper, and ginger.

> ❝ I love a rare rib-eye steak as much as the next man, but nothing can beat beef that has been slowly braised in a carefully balanced stock. The French, of course, are masters of this style of cooking, and at the restaurant we will often braise short ribs with red wine, garlic, and thyme and then serve them with wild mushrooms and bone marrow. But for a very different take, try this recipe—it's a meat eater's delight: a very large chunk of tender beef on the bone packed with Asian flavors. Although the cooking time is lengthy, the actual work involved is minimal. ❞

Asian spiced short ribs

SERVES 4

vegetable oil, for frying

4 short beef ribs, each weighing
    about 1¼ lbs

8 garlic cloves, roughly chopped

6 green bird's eye chiles,
    roughly chopped

1 cup fresh, roughly sliced ginger

1½ tablespoons Chinese
    five-spice powder

5 star anise, bashed up a little
    in a mortar and pestle

1 teaspoon salt

⅓ cup sugar

5 tablespoons soy sauce

1 tablespoon fish sauce

1 tablespoon red wine vinegar

juice of 1 orange

about 3 quarts beef stock

5 lemongrass stalks, bruised
    and frayed

TO SERVE

12 long sprigs of cilantro, stored
    in cold water in the fridge

4 scallions, finely sliced
    on the diagonal

4 red chiles, finely sliced
    on the diagonal

sticky white rice

It's well worth assembling all the ingredients, except for the last three items, before you begin cooking so that you are completely ready.

First, color the short ribs. At this stage you are not trying to cook them at all, just to build up a good caramelization all over. Heat a splash of vegetable oil in a frying pan. Place 2 of the ribs into the pan and cook, turning once, until colored on both sides. Remove from the pan. Repeat with the remaining 2 ribs and set aside.

Heat another splash of vegetable oil in a pot or pan large enough to hold the ribs comfortably. Add the garlic, chiles, and ginger and cook for a minute or two. A small amount of color is okay—not too much! Add the Chinese five-spice powder along with the star anise, salt, and sugar, and give this all a good stir. Add the soy sauce, fish sauce, red wine vinegar, and orange juice—this should immediately sizzle—and boil for a minute.

Pour in the beef stock and add the lemongrass. Carefully place the ribs into the pan—they need to be submerged in stock, so push them to the bottom and add a dash of water if they're still poking above the surface. Reduce the heat to low so that the stock doesn't even simmer (this is very important because if you cook the meat in boiling stock it will tighten and force out the natural juices, leaving you with a great stock but dry meat). Leave to cook for 1½–2 hours or until the meat is really tender. If the level of stock falls well below the beef, top it up with a little water.

Transfer the ribs to a plate to cool. Strain the stock to remove all the bits and return to the pan. Bring to a rapid boil and cook until reduced by half to form a very rich, spicy, and highly aromatic broth, as it shall now be known (because it sounds more Asian and a lot more appealing!). Cool and chill until required if not using right away.

Return the beef to the pan with the boiling broth to warm up. The beef probably won't be submerged in the broth, but that's okay—use tongs to turn the ribs over until they are heated through and nice and tender.

If by chance it's summer and you have a barbecue available, you could reheat the cooked short ribs on the grill—this would add a wonderful smoky flavor.

Place the beef onto a large serving dish and pour on the broth. Drain the cilantro and sprinkle it over the beef, along with the scallions and chiles. Serve with plain sticky white rice.

A WORD ON SHORT RIBS

Short ribs are made up of four or five 10-inch sections of rib bone with a large chunk of meat in between. They are big and bulky, but require little in the way of preparation, apart from cutting into portions. To do this, cut through the middle of the meat that separates the bone so that you end up with a single strip of meat and bone. Bear in mind that the bone is heavy, so you'll need to factor that in when deciding how much to buy. For my four portions here I started with a single four-bone piece weighing 5 lbs. I then cut this into four fairly evenly sized pieces. Any butcher will know what you are after, but some may need a day or two to get it in, so it's worth pre-ordering if you can.

A WORD ON BEEF STOCK

In a professional kitchen beef stock is produced each week as a matter of course. At home, of course, this usually isn't an option, so I tend to use a decent fresh beef stock. I have on occasions just used beef stock cubes and, to be honest, with all the other flavors involved they work just as well.

Okay, you don't have to eat these for supper—in fact some are just as good for lunch—it's just that publishers love a catchy title! I love cooking, but sometimes on a gray and wet Wednesday night, inspiration (and time) are a little hard to come by, so the dishes in this chapter will, I hope, provide you with a few ideas that can be prepared fairly simply without costing a fortune.

Quick & simple
supper spice

66 It's a few pages now since I've had a rant, so I thought one was due... Cooking on TV can be problematic at times. This dish is a case in point. I cooked it on a morning cooking show on which I was a guest chef. Program makers are very eager to cover all bases and they are forever asking for alternative ingredients and options on the chosen dish.

The process begins with a phone call inviting you on to the show...

'Hi, is that Matt Tebbut?'

'No, it's Paul Merrett.'

'So sorry, Paul, my mistake—Matt's busy and we have you down as a backup.'

'Great... thanks.'

'We'd like to get you on the show. The topic is summer food and you can cook whatever you want...'

'Cool. I'll do a slow-baked shoulder of lamb—ideal for the barbecue.'

'No lamb, I'm afraid. Allegra did that two weeks ago.'

'Hmm, did she? I know—paella.'

'Exec. producer says we can't do any more rice dishes on the show.'

'Okay, what about a whole stuffed sea bass with roasted fennel and aioli?'

'That sounds a bit tricky for the average viewer. Some are not that adventurous... can you make a nice salad?'

'They have chosen to watch a cooking program to be fair... but okay, what about a roasted vegetable couscous salad with feta and pomegranate?'

'Oh, perfect—that sounds fantastic. One thing, could you swap the feta for Cheddar in case that's all they have in the fridge?'

'Well, you could, but it wouldn't be the same. Can't they pop out and buy some feta?'

'And what about the pomegranate? Could that be exchanged for anything?'

'Look, you could make it with plastic cheese and canned mandarin oranges if you want, but this version works best.'

And I'm right, this version does work best. It's a really simple supper, which you can customize any way you wish, but this is how it works best. You could make this dish well ahead of time—possibly even the day before—but for best results serve at room temperature, never from the fridge. There are many ways to cook couscous. If you live next door to a North African who has given you her great grandmother's method, use that. If not, mine will work fine. Lastly, a quick word on the vegetables. The recipe title has 'roasted' vegetables, but we aren't going to roast them at all—we are going to cook them in a frying pan on the stove. Menu and recipe writers are allowed a little artistic licence! 99

Roasted vegetable couscous with feta & pomegranate

SERVES 4 AS A MAIN COURSE—A SALAD ON THE SIDE WOULD BE NICE BUT NO NEED FOR MUCH ELSE

CONTINUED... ⟶

Roasted vegetable couscous with feta & pomegranate

CONTINUED FROM PAGE 108

FOR THE COUSCOUS

1½ cups couscous

⅓ cup extra-virgin olive oil

1 teaspoon fennel seeds

2 teaspoons ras-el-hanout

1 teaspoon cumin seeds

1 teaspoon ground turmeric

½ teaspoon red pepper flakes

⅔ teaspoon salt

3 garlic cloves, chopped

¾ cup boiling water

FOR THE "ROASTED" VEGETABLES

about ¾ cup extra-virgin olive oil

1 small eggplant, cut into wedges

1 red onion, cut into wedges

1 red pepper, cut into large dice

1 yellow pepper, cut into large dice

1 head broccoli, cut into small florets

1 small sweet potato, peeled and diced

6 button mushrooms, sliced

TO SERVE

3 plum tomatoes, cut into chunky dice

1⅓ cups feta cheese, broken into chunks

1 cup chopped cilantro

5 mint leaves, chopped

1 pomegranate

1¼ cups extra-virgin olive oil

Tip the couscous into a bowl. Heat the oil in a frying pan until hot but not smoking. Add the spices, salt, and garlic and leave to sizzle for 2 minutes, then add to the bowl with the couscous and mix well. The heat will bring out the flavor of the spices while the oil will help prevent the couscous from clumping up into lumps. Pour the boiling water over the couscous, stir, and immediately cover tightly with plastic wrap. Set aside for 8–10 minutes.

Now for the "roasted" vegetables... all of which should be cooked over medium–high heat until they are just cooked.

EGGPLANT

Heat ¼ cup of the oil in a frying pan and cook the eggplant until dark brown and cooked through (7–8 minutes). Transfer to a plate and set aside.

RED ONION

Pour another 2 tablespoons of the oil into the frying pan and cook the onion until golden brown and softened (3–4 minutes). Tip onto the same plate as the eggplant.

PEPPERS

Add 1 tablespoon more of the oil to the frying pan and cook the peppers until slightly softened and begining to caramelize (2–3 minutes). Transfer to the plate.

BROCCOLI

Heat 2 tablespoons of the oil and cook the broccoli until lightly charred—be brave and let it catch and color (2 minutes). Tip onto the plate.

SWEET POTATO

Cook, using about 2 tablespoons more of the oil, until caramelized and soft (5–6 minutes), then transfer to the plate.

BUTTON MUSHROOMS

Heat the remaining tablespoon of oil and cook the mushrooms until caramelized and soft (3–4 minutes), then add to the cooked veg plate.

Add all of the vegetables into the bowl with the couscous. Fluff up the couscous using a fork, which will also mix in the veg.

To serve, add the tomatoes, feta, and herbs to the couscous and mix. Halve the pomegranate and use a spoon to scoop out the flesh, including any juice, and add to the couscous. Pour in the olive oil and give a final mix. A salad and yogurt dip go well with couscous—the Mint & Mango Yogurt Dip on page 192 would be a winner.

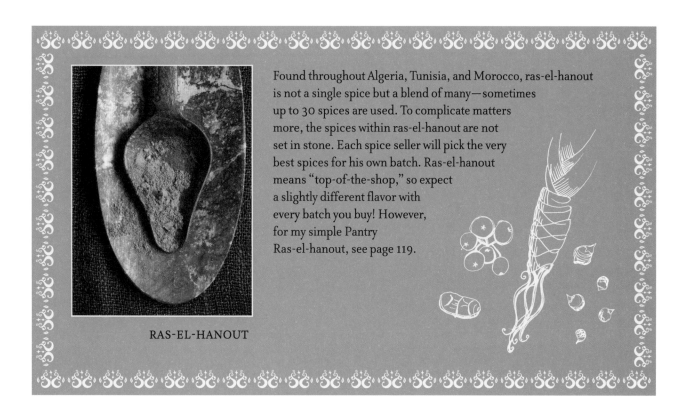

Found throughout Algeria, Tunisia, and Morocco, ras-el-hanout is not a single spice but a blend of many—sometimes up to 30 spices are used. To complicate matters more, the spices within ras-el-hanout are not set in stone. Each spice seller will pick the very best spices for his own batch. Ras-el-hanout means "top-of-the-shop," so expect a slightly different flavor with every batch you buy! However, for my simple Pantry Ras-el-hanout, see page 119.

RAS-EL-HANOUT

66 My first job (way, way back!) was as an apprentice chef at The Ritz London. One of my daily tasks was to make and shape the falafel mix, so popular with the Middle Eastern guests. Prior to this I had never heard of falafel—this was years before it became the trendy food of choice.

Falafel are small, highly flavored, fried nuggets of ground raw chickpeas. They are popular throughout the Middle East, although the actual falafel epicenter is shrouded in mystery. An Egyptian taxi driver kindly informed me that falafel originated in Egypt, while a Lebanese barber was adamant that they were actually first served in Lebanon. Get the picture?

Anyway, I love falafel and I wanted to include a recipe in this book. The problem is I feel a bit mean encouraging you to make these crispy fritters without advising you on ways to use them. The good news is that falafel production can take place on a large scale as they freeze well and can be fried straight from frozen. So here are three falafelly suggestions. (Yes, three! That's three FREE recipes when you think about it—you won't get that in your average cookbook!) I figure this will keep you happily eating falafel for weeks to come. 99

Reasons to make falafel 1, 2 & 3

FOR THE BASIC FALAFEL MIXTURE

2 cups dried chickpeas (never use canned chickpeas because you need the absorption quality of the dried)

3 cups chopped cilantro

1 cup fresh grated ginger

4 red chiles, finely chopped

2 garlic cloves, finely chopped

8 scallions, roughly chopped

good pinch of salt

vegetable oil, for deep-frying

Soak the chickpeas for 6 hours or overnight. Drain and pour into the bowl of a blender or food processor. Add the remaining ingredients and process until the mixture resembles bread crumbs. (Don't blend to a smooth paste because that will inhibit the finished texture.) Shape the falafel according to your chosen recipe (see below). The falafel can be either frozen or fried.

GENERAL FALAFEL-FRYING TIPS

To fry from fresh or frozen, half fill a large, high-sided pan with oil and heat to 350°F. Fry the falafel until deep golden brown in color, carefully remove from the oil using a slotted spoon, drain on paper towel and proceed with your chosen recipe below.

The three reasons

1. FALAFEL BURGERS

These can be shaped by hand; however, I push the mixture inside a pastry cutter to form a perfect burger shape. Fry and serve in a sesame bun with tomato, lettuce, and Tzatziki (see page 182).

2. FALAFEL SALAD

Overfill a teaspoon with falafel mixture. Press the spoon against your palm to form the falafel into a sort of egg shape. Fry and serve warm with a salad involving roasted pepper and eggplant, feta cheese and tomato.

3. FALAFEL WRAP

Roll the falafel mixture into a walnut-sized ball. Fry, then arrange in the center of a tortilla wrap. Top with a little Greek yogurt, finely sliced red onion, grated Cheddar cheese, and shredded lettuce.

❝ Okay, to you and me this is really a grilled cheese sandwich, but, let's face it, quesadilla does sound a lot more exotic! To the professional caterer, that means we can put the price up by at least a buck or two, and for home cooks it means you can serve it to friends without them calling you a cheapskate. A lot of my quesadilla consumption actually takes place between meals as they make a great afternoon snack (not bad as an evening snack, too).

The word "quesadilla" comes from the Spanish for "cheese." It's actually Mexican in origin and, as well as cheese, the other essential ingredient is the flour tortillas, or wraps as they are sometimes called. Beyond that, the world of quesadillas is open to interpretation… ❞

Tomato & scallion quesadilla with three bean, chile & avocado salsa

SERVES 4

8 flour tortillas or wraps

2 cups grated Cheddar cheese

4 large tomatoes, thinly sliced

1 bunch of scallions, finely sliced

2 tablespoons olive oil

FOR THE SALSA

1 cup canned cannellini beans, rinsed and drained

1 cup canned kidney beans, rinsed and drained

1 cup canned chickpeas, rinsed and drained

½ red onion, finely chopped

2 red chiles, finely diced

1 ripe avocado, peeled, stoned and diced

2 tablespoons olive oil

dash of balsamic vinegar

juice of ½ lemon

Lay 4 of the tortillas or wraps onto the work surface and sprinkle with half of the cheese. Layer the tomatoes on top to cover as much of the tortillas as possible. Sprinkle on the scallions and top with the remaining cheese. Place the 4 remaining tortillas on top to form 4 round sandwiches. It's worth mentioning that the cheese glues the wraps together, which is why we put it top and bottom.

Heat ½ a tablespoon of the oil in a frying pan large enough to hold a quesadilla. Lay one in the pan and leave to sizzle for about 2 minutes or until crisp and brown. And now comes the only dramatic moment in quesadilla production—you need to flip it over! The easiest way of doing this is to put a spatula underneath and your hand on the cool top and gently turn it over. Cook on the "B" side for another 2 minutes, then slide out of the pan onto a plate. Repeat with the remaining 3 quesadillas.

To make the salsa, mix the beans and chickpeas together in a bowl and add the onion, chiles, and avocado. Pour in the olive oil, balsamic vinegar, and lemon juice. Scatter this over the quesadillas and serve.

This dish, of course, doesn't have to be frozen—feel free to make the dhal and eat it right there and then—but it can be made in a large batch and put in the freezer, so that you are only a quick ping in the microwave away from a very simple supper. Dhal is a dish eaten all over India, with various regional twists. There is a wide variety of beans that you could use instead of red lentils: chickpeas, green lentils, and yellow split peas all work very well. Dhal like this can be eaten as is, with a simple salad and some flatbread, or you could serve it with a curry.

Paneer is commonly used in Indian cuisine, and most of us probably first encounter it in 'matar paneer,' which pleasingly translates as 'cheesy peas.' The first time I made matar paneer, the only option was to make the cheese myself, but it is now stocked in some supermarkets. If you do feel like a bit of cheese production, see the paneer recipe on page 201.

Red lentil dhal for the freezer

MAKES 8 CUPS OF DHAL, WHICH I FIGURE IS ABOUT 12 MAIN-COURSE PORTIONS

vegetable oil, for frying

3 onions, finely chopped

4 garlic cloves, finely chopped

3-inch piece of fresh ginger, peeled and grated

4 red chiles, finely chopped

½ tablespoon chile powder

2 teaspoons asafetida

1 teaspoon yellow mustard seeds

½ tablespoon ground turmeric

½ tablespoon ground cumin

½ tablespoon cumin seeds

1 tablespoon ground coriander

1½ tablespoons curry powder

1 tablespoon garam masala

2 lbs dried red lentils, rinsed and drained

½ teaspoon salt

14oz can coconut milk

TO SERVE

vegetable oil, for frying

3 sweet potatoes, peeled and diced

14oz paneer

2 cups frozen peas, defrosted

good handful of spinach

2 tablespoons chopped fresh cilantro

Heat the oil in a large pan and cook the onions, garlic, ginger, and chiles until golden brown. Tip in the spices and lentils, stir, and leave everything to sizzle a bit.

Pour in about 8 cups of water to cover the lentils, then add the salt and coconut milk.

Bring to a simmer and cook until the lentils are soft and much of the liquid has been absorbed. There are not hard-and-fast rules here—you are in charge. I like my dhal to be the consistency of Greek yogurt, while my mother's dhal is much thinner, almost sauce-like.

Right, more decisions … At the moment your dhal is very textured because most of the lentils will have swollen and broken. I like this texture, but if you prefer a smooth dhal, grab your immersion blender and purée the contents of the pan. Either way, the dhal is now ready for the freezer.

If you're not freezing it, or if you have defrosted dhal at the ready, here's how to finish it off prior to serving. Warm it in a pan or the microwave. Meanwhile, heat a little oil in a pan and cook the sweet potatoes until caramelized and cooked through. Add to the dhal.

Dice or break up the paneer and cook with a touch of oil until colored on all sides, then add to the dhal. Toss in the peas, spinach, and cilantro. Stir to warm through and serve.

A little while ago, I was asked what would be my desert island dish, and biriyani got the nod. Every two weeks or so I make the short trip to Southall near my home in London for some real Indian food, and I have to force myself to try new dishes rather than order what I really want—a biriyani! In case you don't know, a biriyani is a fragrant concoction of scented rice to which one can add seafood, chicken, or lamb or, as is the case here, keep it vegetarian.

The art of making a good, genuine biriyani can be very complex both in terms of ingredients and method. I certainly encourage you to experiment, but everyone needs a starting point and this is a simple stove-top, weekday supper version that won't challenge your cooking skills to the limit. A word about rice quantities: most recipes generally recommend ¼ cup per serving, but in my house that's never enough, so I've upped it—you won't regret having more!

After-work stovetop biriyani

SERVES 4

1⅔ cups Basmati rice

3 tablespoons vegetable oil

1 large onion, finely sliced

12 button mushrooms, sliced

3 garlic cloves, finely chopped

⅔ cup fresh peeled and grated ginger

2 plum tomatoes, finely chopped

1-inch cinnamon stick

½ teaspoon fennel seeds

½ teaspoon cumin seeds

20 curry leaves

1 tablespoon hot curry powder

½ teaspoon salt

1 cup frozen peas

6 cups broccoli, broken into small florets

1 tablespoon chopped cilantro

Rinse the rice in a sieve under cold running water, drain thoroughly, and set aside.

Heat the oil in a lidded pot roughly 10 inches in diameter and 4 inches deep. Throw in the onion and mushrooms and cook for 5 minutes or until slightly colored. Add the garlic, ginger, and tomatoes and leave to sizzle for 2 minutes or until the moisture from the tomatoes has evaporated. Add the cinnamon, fennel seeds, cumin seeds, curry leaves, and curry powder and cook for a minute or so. Add the rice and salt and very gently stir to mix everything up a little. (Stirring rice causes the grains to release starch, which makes for a gluey, sticky supper, so go carefully. See page 200 for more on cooking rice).

Now you need to add cold water—I haven't given a measurement here because I was taught to cook rice by an elderly Bangladeshi cook and he had an ingenious method. Fill a pitcher with cold water; gently pour it into the pot until it just covers the rice. At this point, put your index finger into the pot (trust me!) with the tip touching the rice, and pour in more water until it reaches the first joint of your finger. This may seem crazy but it works—every time! Bring to a rapid boil. (I didn't mention removing your finger because I guessed you'd realize that!)

Add the peas and broccoli but don't stir. Bring back to a boil. Cover the pot with foil and the lid to trap the steam. Cook for exactly 5 minutes, then switch off the heat and leave well alone for 20 minutes. Don't be tempted to lift the lid or the steam will escape.

After 20 minutes, lift the lid off your perfectly cooked biriyani, fluff up the rice, sprinkle with the cilantro, and serve.

A Moroccan tagine is a slow-cooked stew, named after the clay pot in which it's cooked. This recipe is possibly not as Moroccan as most—it's my make-it-quick-at-home version—so if you don't own a tagine, don't worry, I won't say a word. I have purposely tried to keep the ingredients limited and familiar because it seems wrong to boast that you can cook this in 25 minutes if it takes 3 days to track down authentic yet curious ingredients, such as pigeon, agarwood, or fresh quince.

One spice that you will see mentioned in many tagine recipes is ras-el-hanout, which is actually not one spice at all but a selection of the finest spices a particular supplier has to offer. It is available online, but you will likely have many of the spices contained within sitting in your pantry right now.

Twenty-five-minute (or thereabouts) vegetable tagine with cauliflower couscous

SERVES 4

¾ cup olive oil, divided

1 lb sweet potato, peeled and cut into chunky dice

1 lb new potatoes, thickly sliced

1 yellow pepper, diced

1 red pepper, diced

1 large red onion, cut into 12 wedges

8 garlic cloves, roughly chopped

14oz can chopped tomatoes

pinch of salt

20 pitted green olives

14oz can chickpeas, rinsed and drained

2 cups fresh or frozen lima beans

1 cup dried apricots, halved

1 cauliflower, broken into florets

1 tablespoon sliced almonds, to serve

MY PANTRY RAS-EL-HANOUT

½ tablespoon fennel seeds

large pinch of red pepper flakes

½ tablespoon cumin seeds

1 teaspoon coriander seeds

1-inch cinnamon stick

1 teaspoon ground ginger

½ tablespoon paprika

Okay, we've got to work quickly if we are going to get this done in 25 minutes. Pour ⅓ cup of the olive oil into a pan and cook the sweet potato, new potatoes, peppers, onion, and garlic until they are beginning to color.

While this is going on, prepare the spice mix. Grind the fennel seeds, red pepper flakes, cumin seeds, coriander seeds, and cinnamon in a mortar and pestle, and mix with the ginger and paprika.

Add the spice mix to the pan. Add the chopped tomatoes and pour in up to 2½ cups water, add the salt, and bring to a simmer. Toss in the olives, chickpeas, lima beans, and apricots, and simmer until the potatoes are soft, about 10–12 minutes.

Meanwhile, process the cauliflower to a fine crumb in a blender or food processor until it cunningly resembles couscous. Steam the cauliflower in a fine colander over a pan of boiling water for 5 minutes. (A word on the cauliflower couscous… I wish I had invented this quirky yet clever vegetable accompaniment, but sadly I didn't. I stole it. A few years ago I went to El Bulli in Spain and one of the dishes included cauliflower chopped up and served as coucous. Simple. But ingenious.)

Stir the remaining olive oil into the tagine, sprinkle with the almonds, and serve with the cauliflower couscous.

> If I were to go to a dinner party and be served *just* a bowl of soup, I would probably take the host to one side and deliver a two-minute lecture on menu planning. That said, if I visited the same friend on a Saturday lunchtime and was served a good hearty soup with lots of flavor and crusty bread, I would slap the host on the back and proclaim them a culinary genius. It just goes to show what difference a few hours can make to a cook's reputation!
>
> This is more than just a soup—it's a hearty main course perfect for a weekend brunch (or any other day for that matter!). The trick with this soup is to balance the smooth creamy flavor of the butternut and the coconut milk with the punch of the spice. I tend to use the word chowder to indicate a soup with texture—feel free to blend it as smooth as you wish, but I think the texture allows the individual flavors to shine through.

Butternut chowder with coconut, chile & cilantro

SERVES 8 HUNGRY PEOPLE

2 teaspoons cumin seeds

2 teaspoons fennel seeds

1 teaspoon red pepper flakes

1 teaspoon medium curry powder

6 cups peeled, seeded, and diced butternut squash

vegetable oil, for frying

4 garlic cloves, chopped

2½ cups water

3 cups coconut milk

2 red bird's eye chiles

small bunch of basil

small bunch of cilantro

juice of 1 lime

salt and pepper

Combine the cumin seeds, fennel seeds, red pepper flakes, and curry powder in a large bowl. Add the butternut squash and toss to coat.

Heat the oil in a frying pan and cook the spice-coated butternut, in batches if necessary, until pale golden-brown in color. The point here is to caramelize but not cook it. This caramelization will add another layer of flavor to the finished soup.

Tip the butternut squash into a large pan and toss in the garlic. Pour in the water and coconut milk and bring to a simmer. Cook for 15 minutes or until the butternut squash is soft and cooked through.

Porcess the soup in a blender or food processor, in batches if necessary, or use a hand-held immersion blender. Process until fairly smooth but still with a little texture. If not serving immediately, cool the soup and chill in the fridge or freeze until required.

To serve, bash the bird's eye chiles, basil, and cilantro to a pulp in a mortar and pestle and stir into the chowder. Squeeze in the lime juice and season to taste. Serve with plenty of crusty bread.

66 This vaguely Thai-style curry is one of my favorite quick and easy dishes. The choice of fish is very much up to you—pick something that suits your pocket and tickles your fancy. The last time I made this, I used whole gutted bream and cut it straight through the body and backbone into chunks. If you prefer your fish boneless, buy fillets, but in this style of dish they may break up a little. 99

A quick spicy fish curry

SERVES 4

2 x 1 lb sea bream, scaled, gutted
    and heads removed

1½ tablespoons vegetable oil

3 shallots, sliced into rings

1 garlic clove, finely chopped

½ cup peeled and grated fresh ginger

2 teaspoons hot curry powder

2 x 14oz cans coconut milk

½ teaspoon salt

2 lemongrass stalks

6 kaffir lime leaves

4 heads of bok choy, halved

1 tablespoon soy sauce, or to taste

3 teaspoons fish sauce, or to taste

1 bunch of basil

juice of 1 lime

Cut the bream through the bone into chunks and set aside.

Heat the oil in a pan over low to medium heat and cook the shallots, garlic, and ginger until slightly softened. Add the curry powder and stir, then pour in the coconut milk, add the salt, and bring to a simmer.

Meanwhile, bash the lemongrass and lime leaves in a mortar and pestle until the lemongrass is bruised and frayed.

Throw the lemongrass and lime leaves into the pan and simmer gently for 10 minutes. Add the bream, ensuring that the liquid covers the fish—if not, add a splash of water. Bring back to a simmer and cook very gently for 10 minutes. Add the bok choy, ensuring it is submerged, and cook for another 5 minutes or until the bream is cooked through.

Add the soy and fish sauce. Taste and add more if you wish. Just before serving, bash up the basil in a mortar and pestle and stir into the stew. Squeeze in the lime juice and serve with sticky rice.

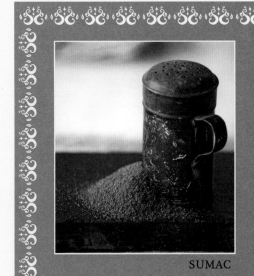

SUMAC

Sumac is a deep red, fairly granular powder used extensively in North African and Middle Eastern cuisine. I tend to use it more as a condiment rather than adding it during the cooking of a dish. Leave a small bowl on the table and allow people to help themselves. It's great sprinkled over grilled meat skewers or used to pep up a braised dish. The flavor is best described as peppery with a bit of a citrus twang.

66 This is the perfect pasta dish. A bit of a modern classic in the pasta world, I'd say. Light, healthy, easy, and very tasty. I admit that shrimp don't make it the cheapest dish, but it's worth the money. You could substitute the pappardelle with other pasta shapes and sizes, if you like. I buy decent-quality dried pappardelle made in the traditional way using whole eggs. If you'd like to make your own, your pasta dish will taste even better than mine. 99

Shrimp pappardelle with chile, lemon, garlic, basil & parsley

SERVES 4 (ACTUALLY IT MAY EVEN STRETCH TO 5 BECAUSE I ALWAYS COOK MORE THAN THE RECOMMENDED AMOUNT OF PASTA PER PERSON AND WE NEVER HAVE ANY LEFT OVER!)

1 lb dried pappardelle

⅔ cup best-quality extra-virgin olive oil

20 peeled raw extra-large shrimp (save the shells for the Shrimp and Coconut Bisque on page 35)

3 chiles, finely chopped

3 garlic cloves, finely chopped

12 basil leaves, torn

2 tablespoons coarsely chopped flat-leaf parsley

grated zest of ½ lemon

good pinch of sea salt flakes

freshly ground black pepper

Bring a large pan of water to a boil (I don't add salt or oil when cooking pasta but I've met Italians who do, so it's your call) and cook the pasta according to the package instructions, carefully loosening the clump of pasta into ribbons using a large fork after about a minute. Drain the pasta through, put it back into the pan, and pour in about half of the olive oil. It will last like this, happily, for 10 minutes or so, allowing you to do the next part.

Heat a little of the remaining oil in a nonstick frying pan over high heat. Toss in the shrimp and cook hard and fast for about 90 seconds on each side, or until pinkish-red with a roasty look and aroma. Reduce the heat to low and add the rest of the oil, the chiles, and garlic. Sizzle for 30 seconds, tip into the pan of drained pasta, and gently mix through.

Toss in the basil leaves. Add the parsley, lemon zest, and salt and a twist or three of pepper. Serve immediately, perhaps alongside an arugula salad.

By the way, all the Italians I know tell me it's very bad form to put grated Parmesan on seafood pasta (and risottos, too). While not wishing to come across as a heathen, or indeed cause a diplomatic incident, I say if you want cheese, you go ahead and have it.

Chermoula is a North African spicy paste or marinade very often, though not exclusively, used in fish dishes. There are hundreds of versions, from Morocco to Algeria to Tunisia, and each one is slightly different but usually involves cumin seeds, garlic, preserved lemon, and some herbs along the way. Although I'm a well-traveled guy, the nearest I've got to North Africa is a Moroccan food store in London.

Many years ago, as a budding young chef trying his hand at television, I spent a day inside this Moroccan food store, with the owner, making a short film about spices. Toward the end of the day we cooked a lamb tagine with dates on a camping stove outside his shop, then jumped on passersby, forcing them to try the tagine and say nice things into the camera. They all obliged, as people minding their own business tend to do when accosted by a chef and a camera crew. All, that is, except the owner of the store.

He had sold us the ingredients (at a huge profit!) for the tagine, but when asked to taste, it he screwed up his face in obvious disappointment—obligingly all on camera! I was disappointed and, sensing this, he beckoned me through the shop to a small kitchen where he was cooking fish *à la chermoula* for his supper. We sat and ate this as he explained, very clearly, that I should never again attempt to cook Moroccan food. So for the miserable guy who derailed my TV career before it had even started, here is your recipe... in my book (ha ha). I begrudgingly admit it tastes amazing. You won't like the salad—I invented it.

Please don't feel you have to use mackerel if it's not your kind of fish—any would work well, but I think oily mackerel is particularly good with the preserved lemon and paprika.

Mackerel chermoula on a roasted butternut salad

SERVES 4

4 very fresh, decent-sized
    mackerel fillets

olive oil, for cooking

FOR THE CHERMOULA PASTE

1 teaspoon coriander seeds

1 teaspoon cumin seeds

2 garlic cloves, crushed to a paste

good pinch of saffron

2 tablespoons finely chopped
    flat-leaf parsley

2 tablespoons finely
    chopped cilantro

½ teaspoon salt

½ teaspoon paprika

1 small red bird's eye chile,
    very finely chopped

2 preserved lemons, skin only,
    very finely chopped

2 tablespoons olive oil

FOR THE SALAD

2 tablespoons olive oil

½ butternut squash, peeled and diced

handful of arugula leaves

8 cherry tomatoes, cut in wedges

4 scallions, finely sliced on
    an angle

seeds from ½ pomegranate

splash of balsamic vinegar

To make the chermoula paste, heat a frying pan and dry-fry the coriander seeds and cumin seeds. Leave to cool, then grind to a powder in a mortar and pestle. Tip into a bowl.

Add the garlic, saffron, parsley, cilantro, salt, paprika, chile and preserved lemon. Stir well, then mix in the olive oil.

Spoon half of the chermoula paste into a dish and lay the mackerel fillets on top. Spoon the remaining paste over the top to cover the fish. Leave to marinate for 15 minutes.

To make the salad, heat the oil in a frying pan over a medium-high heat, tip in the butternut squash and cook until golden brown and cooked through (5–6 minutes). Transfer to a bowl and add the arugula, tomatoes, and scallions. Using a spoon, dig out the pomegranate seeds from the skin and add to the salad. Add a splash of balsamic vinegar and arrange on four serving plates.

When you're ready to cook the fish, heat the oil in a nonstick frying pan over high heat. Place the mackerel fillets, skin-side down, into the pan and cook for 3–4 minutes or until the skin has colored. Flip the mackerel over and cook for another 3–4 minutes or until the fish is cooked through.

Toward the end of the cooking time, tip any remaining chermoula into the frying pan with the mackerel and spoon it over the fish when you serve.

Place the mackerel fillets on top of the salad and serve.

" This recipe won't win any awards for authenticity or creative genius, but I think it's worthy of inclusion in this chapter simply because it's a very basic, quick, and simple curry base that can be frozen and used as and when curry is required. Just to get you going, I've included a simple recipe below for spicy chicken thighs as a suggestion for using the basic sauce (a free gift from me), but you could also use it with meatballs, diced chicken, fish, or chunks of your favorite vegetables. "

A basic curry sauce for the freezer, which could become ...

MAKES 12 PORTIONS

3 tablespoons vegetable oil

4 onions, very finely diced

8 garlic cloves, finely chopped

¾ cup fresh peeled and grated ginger

3 tablespoons hot curry powder

2 x 14oz cans chopped tomatoes

1 cup chicken or vegetable stock

Heat the oil in a pan over medium heat. Add the onions, garlic, and ginger and cook for 25 minutes or until caramelized and dark brown in color, stirring frequently. Don't rush this stage or they will burn—remember: dark brown, not black! If the onions stick, add 1 teaspoon water and stir vigorously to work the stuck bits back into the bulk.

Add the curry powder and cook for 5 minutes. Add the tomatoes and cook for another 10 minutes or until the liquid from the tomatoes has evaporated.

Pour in the stock and bring to a simmer. Cook for another 10 minutes or until thickened. Cool and freeze in freezer bags or plastic containers until required (I usually divide the sauce into 3 so each batch will serve 4 people).

Below is one meal you could make from your curry base.

...Spicy chicken thighs with chickpeas & cilantro

SERVES 4

vegetable oil, for frying

8 chicken thighs or drumsticks

⅓ quantity Basic Curry Sauce, defrosted

14oz can coconut milk or 1¼ cups water

14oz can chickpeas, rinsed and drained

good handful of baby spinach

1 tablespoon chopped cilantro

Heat the oil in a frying pan over medium heat and cook the chicken pieces until golden-brown all over.

Meanwhile, pour the Basic Curry Sauce into a pan. Add the coconut milk or water, stir well, and bring to a simmer.

Add the chicken pieces to the simmering sauce and cook for 30 minutes, or until cooked through. Add the chickpeas and cook for another 5 minutes.

Stir in the spinach and cilantro and serve with Basmati rice.

66 I won't yabber on about the Queen's coronation, because whenever a version of this dish is published we get the same old history lesson. Suffice to say that this is the perfect summer lunch—spicy, creamy, easy-to-make, it just checks all the boxes. Serve it as part of a buffet, heap it on top of baked potatoes, dot small spoonfuls onto broken pieces of poppadom as a canapé, or serve it with a crusty baguette at a royal celebration. It's your call.

As already acknowledged, this is certainly not the first cookbook to include Coronation Chicken. However, I think a lot of recipes are too sweet and cloying, or they recommend cooking diced chicken breast, meaning that the sauce is never properly incorporated into the chicken. Roasting a whole chicken is definitely the way forward. So I'm giving you my favorite version created by Mrs. Merrett (the Elder). 99

Coronation chicken

SERVES 4

1 freshly roasted chicken

vegetable oil, for frying

2 shallots

1 garlic clove

¼ cup grated fresh ginger

2 tomatoes, finely diced

1 tablespoon hot curry powder

3 tablespoons mango chutney

⅔ cup chicken stock

1¼ cups mayonnaise

3 tablespoons coconut cream

pinch of salt

1 tablespoon chopped cilantro

Let's presume you know how to roast a chicken, and that you've got it cooking right now. It just makes my job easier. When it comes out of the oven, leave it to cool.

Heat the vegetable oil in a pan and toss in the shallots, garlic, and ginger. Sizzle away until slightly colored. Throw in the tomatoes and cook until any liquid has evaporated. Stir in the curry powder and mango chutney.

Pour in the stock, bring to a simmer, and cook gently for 10 minutes. For a smooth curry mayonnaise, strain the mixture. I don't bother because I like the texture (yes, yes... and I'm lazy). Leave to cool completely before stirring in the mayonnaise and coconut cream.

Back to the chicken. Remove the meat from the carcass, slicing any large pieces up a little. Spoon in the curry mayonnaise and mix well. Taste and season with salt, then just before serving mix in the cilantro.

Chicken tandoori wrap in flower pot (or not)

SERVES 4

4 boneless, skinless chicken breasts

2-inch piece of fresh ginger, peeled and grated

4 garlic cloves, chopped

2 green chiles, chopped

3 tablespoons roughly chopped cilantro

½ tablespoon roughly chopped mint

juice of ½ lemon

½ cup Greek yogurt

1 teaspoon ground coriander

1 teaspoon ground cumin

½ teaspoon chile powder

1 teaspoon garam masala

¼ teaspoon ground black pepper

vegetable oil, for frying

4 whole-wheat naan breads

2 Boston lettuces, finely shredded

1 red onion, sliced

Using a sharp knife, slash each chicken breast 5 times to create shallow, diagonal cuts (essential for allowing the marinade to really penetrate the chicken). Transfer to a large bowl and set aside.

Next up is the marinade. Process the ginger, garlic, chiles, cilantro, mint, lemon juice, and yogurt in a blender or food processor until smooth. Add the ground coriander, cumin, chile powder, garam masala, and pepper and process again to combine. Add to the chicken and mix well to coat the chicken thoroughly, then cover and chill in the fridge for at least an hour—longer would be better (I often do this in the morning and leave it marinating while I'm at work, ready for when I get home).

To cook the chicken, heat a good glug of oil in a large, nonstick, heavy-bottomed frying pan over high heat. Remove any excess marinade from the chicken and cook, in batches if necessary, hard and fast, for 2–3 minutes or until well colored. Don't be tempted to move the pan around or turn the chicken over during this time as it's really important that the chicken gets the full heat from the pan. Flip the chicken over and cook the "B" side until cooked through.

Warm the naan in a grill pan and lay flat on the plate (the naan, not you). Slice the chicken and arrange in the centers of the naan. Add the lettuce and red onion, roll up, and eat!

66 A tandoor is a clay oven used for cooking meat and baking bread. Its origins are thought to be Indian, but tandoors are now widely used throughout Asian cooking. Nowadays high-tech commercial versions are popular, but in its most basic form, a tandoor really amounts to a simple clay pot in which charcoal is burned. The idea is that the food is exposed to the fire itself, thus taking on a fantastic charred flavor and appearance. It's a characteristic virtually impossible to achieve with our conventional home ovens. My local Indian restaurateur informs me that any dish that is cooked in this way and called "tandoori" is always a big seller.

A quick look on the internet will result in lots of tandoor ovens available to purchase for home use, but none of them is cheap, so I've invented a beginner's model to get you started. This seemingly simple oven represents a major achievement in my life. Believe me, I have a nerve trying to teach anybody to build anything. In the "man-who-makes-stuff" department, I am a crushing disappointment.

In life there appear to be two distinct categories of men. There are the real men who make stuff—cupboards, kitchen units, or tree houses for their children. This type of man paints his own house, can easily change the tire on his family car, and would even climb a ladder to fix a leaking roof. And then there are the men who invest in a nation's economy by paying (cash-in-hand, if possible) a semi-professional local man from the former group to carry out these jobs on their behalf.

Rarely does a man from one group join the other, but I have achieved this with my homemade tandoor oven.

Anyway, enough of this self-help bravado rubbish. Let's get your oven up and running. I've written the following instructions like a recipe, just so that we can all understand and follow them more easily! 99

Make your very own tandoor oven

KIT REQUIRED

1 metal garbage pail with lid

4 house bricks

drill (borrow this from a friend if, like me, you don't own one)

length of steel pipe (mine was about 12 inches long and an inch in diameter, and I bought it from the only store in my neighborhood I'd never been in— the hardware store)

about 100 lbs soil

1 very large sturdy clay flowerpot with a hole in the base (mine was about 15 inches in diameter at the top, with a 7-inch diameter base, and it was about 14 inches deep)

a bag of charcoal

fire lighters

a few long metal kebab-type skewers

The first job is the trickiest. You need to drill a hole in the center of the base of the garbage pail. My neighbor (annoyingly capable) pointed out that I should put the garbage pail on the bricks before doing this so that I didn't drill straight through the decking he laid in my garden two years ago. The hole needs to be wide enough to allow the pipe to poke through—another reason why the garbage pail needs to stand on bricks.

Hold the pipe in place so that one end pokes an inch or so through the drilled hole. The other end will just reach the hole in the base of the flower pot—this will create a stream of air to feed the fire once we are up and running. Using the soil, backfill the garbage pail around the pipe to hold it in position.

When the soil reaches the top of the pipe, place your flower pot in the garbage pail. As a guide, you want the lip of the pot to be at the same height as the top lip of the garbage pail. It's very important that you pack as much soil as firmly around and below the flowerpot as possible.

You now have a large flower pot firmly encased in soil in a garbage pail. There should be a metal pipe traveling from the base of the flower pot down through the soil and out of the base of the garbage pail. We are nearly there.

Using the charcoal and fire lighter, get a decent-sized fire going within the flower pot. In my experiments I wasn't brave enough with fire size to start with, and as a result I struggled to build up the temperature of the oven. Feed the initial fire with extra coals so that a third of the flower pot is eventually filled with coals that are glowing red with a powdery gray surface.

Place the lid on the garbage pail and allow the temperature to build up.

Back in the kitchen, prepare a trial skewer—chicken with a simple spicy marinade will do. Cook this by standing the end of the skewer into the fire so that the chicken part is just above the hot coals. Place the lid back on and give it a good 5 minutes, or as long as it takes to cook the meat thoroughly. Eat said chicken and wonder at your achievement. The Chicken Tandoori recipe on page 129 will taste amazing cooked this way.

My own tandoor cooking has since developed. I have twisted and bent an old wire rack to make a grid, which can sit over the charcoal within the pot, so I can cook small chunks of meat or fish.

Put lid on when coals are lit

Clay flowerpot

Coals

Steel pipe

Top up soil when flowerpot is in place

First load of soil

Pipe coming through drilled hole

Bhuna is a dish found on many Indian menus. It indicates meat that has been rubbed with spice and dry-fried. The meat cooks in just the juice it yields rather than having a thick sauce added. I'm rather taken with this particular cooking style, and on your behalf I have visited a vast array of Indian restaurants to sample their particular take on the bhuna. Don't thank me—there are worse jobs...

The following recipe is really three or four different recipes that I have finely chopped, whisked well and rolled out as one. Once you have marinated the chicken there are a few options when it comes to actually eating the stuff. Here are three:

1. Toss the warm cooked chicken with mixed lettuce, tomato, torn-up naan bread, grilled zucchini, and red onion and call it lunch.

2. Lay the cooked chicken onto a tortilla wrap with some shredded lettuce, scallion, and avocado. Roll it up and call it a snack.

3. Serve the warm chicken over a heap of Basmati rice perhaps, with some lime pickle, and call it supper.

Chicken bhuna

SERVES 4

4 chicken breasts, each cut into
    about 10 strips
vegetable oil, for frying

FOR THE MARINADE

6 tablespoons plain yogurt
juice of 1 lemon
2 garlic cloves, very finely chopped
1 teaspoon ground turmeric
$\frac{1}{2}$ tablespoon paprika
4 cardamom pods, seeds only
$\frac{1}{2}$ teaspoon salt
$\frac{1}{2}$ teaspoon chile powder
$1\frac{1}{2}$ teaspoons ground cumin

TO SERVE

1 teaspoon garam masala
1 tablespoon chopped cilantro
1 teaspoon chopped fresh mint

First make the marinade. Spoon the yogurt into a bowl and stir in the remaining marinade ingredients. Add the chicken and stir to coat. Chill and allow to marinate, or... see note below.

Heat a little oil in a nonstick frying pan over high heat. Allow the pan and oil to get nice and hot. Remove any excess marinade from the chicken and fry, in manageable batches, until caramelized and cooked through—about 6–8 minutes. (The secret here is patience and trust. If you immediately start moving the pan, or the chicken, around you will lose heat from the pan, the chicken won't caramelize and you'll be left with soggy chicken.) Remove the chicken from the pan and keep warm while you cook the remaining batches.

To serve, sprinkle the garam masala, cilantro, and mint over the chicken and mix to combine. Choose option 1, 2 or 3 from the introduction above and get chomping.

A NOTE ON MARINATING THE CHICKEN

Ideally I would allow the chicken to marinate for about 2 hours. However, having cooked this dish for the last three evenings in a row (to test various recipe nuances), it appears that marinating times can annoy the home cook. My wife, for one, seems to feel that we chefs just write in information about marinating willy-nilly for our own amusement, and that actually it can be overlooked if deemed necessary. As a result we have cooked this bhuna within 5 minutes of mixing the chicken into the yogurt, and we have also left it overnight and cooked it the next day. Both ways tasted fine, which annoyingly means she may be right. Again. So the choice is yours.

In the good old days, serious cookbooks used to employ a quaint system of awarding 'chef's hats' to indicate the technical ability required to make the dish. I have some of these books and I still don't dare attempt the three-hat dishes, just in case I get halfway in and am asked to perform some culinary backflip of which I'm incapable.

I've opted out of employing such a system, but if I had to grade this dish it would only get half a hat—it's that easy.

Bear in mind that, because this meal is supposed to be quick and simple without too much fuss, if you don't have the spices to make my spice rub, start experimenting with your own spice reserves. It's well worth writing down which spices are in the finished mix so that you can make it again if it's a success, or avoid a similar combination if not. Rubs are a great way of using up old jars of spices, and they really can be assembled from any collection of spices. Some assortments work better than others, and if you have a decent cook coming for dinner, I suggest testing your spice rub first to avoid any mishaps.

Salsas turn up in many dishes across the globe, but particularly those with a Spanish influence. There are some culinary rules to a salsa—they should be sharp/sour through the use of citrus, they should be slightly salty, and they should have a spicy kick—but I tend to use the term salsa for a pile of ingredients that I couldn't be bothered to cook! Mix in some lime juice, olive oil, and a pinch of salt and call it a salsa. It works for me.

Spice-rubbed chicken with avocado, mango & red onion salsa

SERVES 4

2 tablespoons light olive oil, plus extra for frying

1 garlic clove, crushed to a paste

4 skin-on boneless chicken breasts

pita bread, to serve

FOR THE SPICE RUB

5 teaspoons ground coriander

7 teaspoons ground cumin

2 teaspoons cracked black pepper

2 teaspoons ground mace

2 teaspoons ground ginger

5 teaspoons cayenne pepper

2 teaspoons table salt

FOR THE SALSA

1 red onion, diced

1 ripe mango, peeled, pitted and diced

1 red pepper, diced

1 avocado, peeled, stoned and diced

20 cilantro leaves, shredded

10 mint leaves, shredded

2 tablespoons light olive oil

juice of ½ lime

To make the spice rub, simply mix all of the ingredients together and pour into an old jar. Label it "Paul Merrett's Mighty Fine Spice Rub" and store in a prominent position in your pantry.

To make the marinade, spoon 3 tablespoons of the spice rub into a large bowl and pour in 2 tablespoons of the oil. Add the garlic, mix to a paste, and set aside.

Using a sharp knife, slash each chicken breast 5 times to create shallow diagonal cuts (essential for allowing the marinade to really penetrate the chicken). Add to the bowl with the marinade and rub all over to coat.

Heat a heavy-bottomed frying or grill pan over high heat. Pour a little oil onto a piece of paper towel and very carefully wipe the inside of the hot pan.

Lay the chicken into the pan, skin-side down, and leave to cook for 4 minutes or until colored. Flip the chicken over and cook for 4 minutes or until cooked through. Transfer to a plate and set aside to rest.

Meanwhile, make the salsa. Toss the onion, mango, pepper and avocado into a bowl. Add the cilantro and mint, pour in the olive oil, squeeze in the lime juice, and mix carefully, ensuring you don't crush the mango or avocado.

Place the chicken onto a serving dish, heap the salsa over the top and serve with pita bread. For added decadence, offer a dollop of tzatziki, too— funnily enough I have a recipe on page 182!

A WORD ON THE MARINADE

There are two basic types of marinade. There is the very wet marinade, into which you plunge meat or fish. The protein is left soaking up the marinade and at some point you remove it, shake off the excess moisture, and start the cooking process. This sort of marinade needs time for the soaking and absorption of flavor.

The other type of marinade is one that stays on the meat or fish while it cooks, usually in the form of a spice paste. This sort of marinating does not require the time factor as the meat or fish carries the marinade right through the cooking process. This dish uses this type of marinade, so if you're reading this minutes before you need to put a meal on the table you're in luck…well, if you have a spare mango and avocado lying around, that is.

❝ Two Tuesdays ago I drank far too much beer. I was out with a couple of friends, both of whom are chefs, and as we staggered out of the pub at closing time one of them suggested that it would be 'sensible' to head home via the Middle Eastern take-out place. I chose a dish called arayes kafta. The next morning I made two solemn pledges—to never ever drink beer again, and to revisit that Middle Eastern take-out and eat the same thing, but this time without the preceding 10 beers. I've kept one of the two pledges—I've been back to the take-out and eaten arayes kafta, which again really hit the spot, but this time I was sober enough to remember exactly what I'd eaten.

So much Middle Eastern cuisine is interwoven and reinterpreted from country to country, but Lebanon appears to get the credit for arayes kafta. Basically it's a toasted sandwich with a spicy meat stuffing. Many recipes ask you to use baharat spice, which you can track down on the internet, but basically baharat is an Arabic spice blend that can be made using spices you may well already have in your pantry. This makes a great barbecue meal, an easy hot light lunch, or the most incredible dish ever eaten by a drunk guy at a bus stop. ❞

Spiced lamb in toasted pita with tomato & red onion salad

SERVES 4

1 lb ground lamb

1 onion, very finely chopped

2 garlic cloves, finely chopped

1 teaspoon salt

1 tablespoon chopped flat-leaf parsley

⅓ cup pine nuts, toasted and ground

1 teaspoon lemon juice

4 pita breads

1 tablespoon olive oil

FOR THE BAHARAT SPICE

8 cardamom seeds

1 teaspoon coriander seeds

1 teaspoon cumin seeds

2 cloves

1 teaspoon ground allspice

½ teaspoon ground black pepper

½ teaspoon ground cinnamon

pinch of freshly grated nutmeg

½ teaspoon chile powder

TO SERVE

tomato wedges

red onion slices

chopped flat-leaf parsley

olive oil

lemon juice

To make the baharat spice, grind the cardamom, coriander and cumin seeds, and the cloves to a powder in a mortar and pestle. Tip into a bowl and add the remaining spices. Mix everything up, transfer to a jar, and store until needed.

Put the ground lamb into a bowl and add the onion, garlic, salt, 2 teaspoons of the baharat spice, the parsley, pine nuts, and lemon juice. Mix well and use your hands to squelch and squeeze everything together.

Slice the pita breads open and put a decent dollop of the lamb mixture inside each one, flattening the mixture to a thickness of less than an inch. Close the pitas and push down so that the meat is fully covered by the bread.

Heat a grill pan over medium heat and add the oil. Gently cook the pita sandwiches on both sides until the pita is nicely toasted and the meat inside is cooked through.

Serve with a simple salad of tomato wedges, red onion, and flat-leaf parsley dressed with olive oil and lemon juice.

Back in my Michelin-star chef days, I would have wept if I had been asked to make a customer a burger. The irony, of course, is that I'm sure I happily ate my share of burgers during those pompous times—I just would never have agreed to cook one!

Nowadays, in my laid-back gastro pub reincarnation, I send out hundreds of them each week! My butcher makes our burgers by hand, using finest Aberdeen Angus beef, and they are very popular.

Every now and then we change from the traditional beef burger to this one, its exotic North African inspired cousin, the spicy lamb burger.

You will be keen to point out that tzatziki is traditionally made with cucumber, while I am using zucchini. Zucchini works well since it has a little less moisture than cucumber, and thus the texture is improved, I think. If, like me, you are a grow-your-own type, you will know that every year you are in for loads of zucchini, so having one more recipe to use them up is no bad thing.

My Tomato Chile Jam (page 190) goes perfectly with this burger.

Moroccan spiced lamb burger with tomato chile jam & zucchini tzatziki

SERVES 4

1 lb ground lamb
½ onion, very finely chopped
2 garlic cloves, very finely chopped
1 teaspoon ground cumin
1 teaspoon ground coriander
pinch of salt
½ teaspoon paprika

FOR THE TZATZIKI
2 medium zucchini
about 20 mint leaves, shredded
2 garlic cloves, finely chopped
½ cup Greek yogurt

TO SERVE
4 white burger buns
Tomato Chile Jam (see page 190)
lettuce, sliced red onion, and sliced
    cheese (optional)

Strictly speaking, one would make the Tomato Chile Jam first, but we'll kick off with the burger, as it's the "headline act," so to speak.

Put the ground lamb, onion, garlic, cumin, coriander, salt, and paprika into a bowl and use your hands to mix everything together really well, squishing and squeezing to combine all the flavors. Mold the mixture into four burgers of similar size and chill in the fridge until you are ready to cook.

Next the tzatziki. Grate the zucchini on the coarse side of a box grater. Gently squeeze out any excess moisture and combine with the mint, garlic, and yogurt. Mix well and chill in the fridge until required.

Grill the burgers for about 4 minutes on either side or until cooked to your liking.

Split the buns and toast in a grill pan to give them a pleasing criss-cross look.

Build each burger with a very decent blob of Tomato Chile Jam followed by the tzatziki. Feel free to customize your burger with lettuce, red onion, and even a slice of cheese, if you wish.

Most French restaurants will at some time offer a steak au poivre on their menu. They often use a prime cut of beef for this dish, serving with it a punchy peppercorn sauce. As well as the peppercorns, the other feature of a steak 'au poivre' is the addition of cognac. It's never the cheapest menu option! Here I'm using all of the same tricks but bringing the price down through the use of a prime pork chop and a glug of brandy—this is the quick and simple supper section after all! I'm also going to use soft, fresh green peppercorns rather than the dried black version. These can be found in many Asian stores and indeed the occasional supermarket. They are sold clustered on a vine. I would urge you to make the stock using a dark meat-based cube—I would mix it at double the recommended strength. Using a dark stock cube (beef perhaps) will embellish the flavor and will give the finished sauce a nice milky-coffee color.

Pork chop "au poivre" with wilted spinach

SERVES 4

4 pork chops—for really decent meat look for phrases such as "rare breed," "higher welfare," or "organic"

1 tablespoon vegetable oil

2 large shallots, finely diced

1oz picked, fresh green peppercorns, lightly crushed in a mortar and pestle

about 4 tablespoons brandy

¾ cup strong stock

1¼ cups heavy cream

10oz spinach

pinch of salt

The only preparation required for the pork chops is to use the tip of the knife to cut through the fat several times (as shown in the photograph). This will improve the caramelization of the fat. On no account should you remove the fat—it's the best part.

Heat the vegetable oil in a large frying pan over high heat and lay in the pork chops. Don't cram them in the pan as it will lose heat and they won't color—if your pan is small, perhaps do only 2 at a time. Allow the pork chops to sizzle away for 4–5 minutes and then turn them over for another 4–5 minutes, by which time they will have caramelized nicely and cooked through but will still be juicy. Before you remove them from the pan, use your tongs to stand them on the fatty side so that the fat caramelizes, renders slightly, and crisps up. Remove the pork chops from the frying pan and rest.

Next make the sauce in the same pan—don't wipe the pan out. Any residue merely adds to the flavor. If there is no oil left in the pan, add a tiny bit more. Chuck in the shallots and sizzle until lightly colored. Add the crushed green peppercorns and again sizzle for 1 minute. Pour in the brandy and allow it to boil. If you now pull the pan back over the gas burner, your brandy will catch alight, causing an eyebrow-singeing flame to leap up. This has little effect on the finished dish but does look seriously impressive. Pour in the stock, return to a rapid boil, and reduce by about half the original volume. Pour in the cream and boil again for 2 minutes. Turn the heat down to a simmer and allow the creamy sauce to reduce and thicken slightly. Once you're happy with the consistency, the sauce is ready.

Finally cook the spinach. Heat a saucepan over high heat. Tip in the spinach and let it wilt and soften. The water left on the leaves from washing the spinach is all the moisture it requires to cook. Add the pinch of salt.

Place some spinach on each person's plate. Take the plate of resting pork and put a pork chop on top of the spinach. Pour any juice from the pork plate into the finished sauce and ladle over the pork chops to serve.

I recently found myself cooking in the Maldives for a couple of weeks. When I say "found myself," it sounds as though I may have been the victim of the best kidnapping ever... 'Grabbed during the hours of darkness on a cold, gray, wet night, I was bundled into a car by three ladies in grass skirts and bikinis, taken to the airport, and flown to a Maldivian island surrounded by white sand, coral reef, and crystal blue waters. There I was forced to live in a six-roomed wooden villa on stilts in the sea. Each day I had to cook using only the freshest tropical ingredients including lobsters, crab, tuna, herbs, spices, coconut milk—I was relieved when my wife paid the ransom...'

The point of mentioning the Maldives is to tell you how this dish came into being. Woks, griddles, planchas, and grills were used for most of the cooking, apart from the steaks. Specially flown in from Australia, these were cooked on a large, flat, very hot stone. The meat was cooked very quickly on either side and then allowed to rest until just done.

On my days off I was a guest and therefore entitled to eat the steak. The problem was, I was always too full of lobster, crab and shrimp from the grill to even contemplate attacking a steak. You are probably beginning to realize how tough an assignment this trip to the Maldives was. I mentioned to my kitchen team that I was having problems getting around to eating the steak so, after service on my last night, the boys cooked up a kitchen feast, and here it is...

A WORD ON THE HOT STONE

I don't have one of these at home, and I'm guessing you may not either. The next best thing is definitely a heavy-bottomed cast-iron pan or grill pan, or one of those fancy ceramic plates that heat up in the oven and are then used to sear things (no, I don't have one of those either!).

Smoky beef & green vegetable stir fry

SERVES 4

2 x 7oz sirloin, rib-eye or rump steaks

FOR THE MARINADE

3 tablespoons soy sauce

3 tablespoons sweet chile sauce

1 tablespoon Tabasco

1 tablespoon brown sugar

½ tablespoon fish sauce

juice of ½ lime

The first thing to do is assemble the very simple marinade. Find a bowl big enough to hold the steaks and mix together the soy sauce, sweet chile sauce, Tabasco, brown sugar, fish sauce, and lime juice.

Using a very sharp knife, slash each steak several times to create shallow, diagonal cuts (essential for allowing the marinade to really penetrate the meat). Turn over and repeat. Place the meat into the bowl and rub well with the marinade. Leave to marinate while you prepare the rest of the ingredients.

MORE INGREDIENTS OVERLEAF ...

CONTINUED... ⟶

Smoky beef & green vegetable stir fry

CONTINUED FROM PAGE 143

vegetable oil, for cooking

2 tablespoons sesame oil

1 broccoli head, cut into miniature florets

about 20 sugar snap peas, sliced on an angle

1 green pepper, thinly sliced

about 10 snow peas, sliced into strips

6 scallions, cut into long slices on an angle

1 Boston lettuce, cut into wedges

½ cup chopped cilantro

2 green chiles, thinly sliced

4 garlic cloves, finely chopped

1-inch piece of fresh ginger, peeled and grated

15 picked, fresh green peppercorns, lightly crushed (available in Asian supermarkets; if you can't find them, buy a can of green peppercorns in brine)

1 star anise, ground to a powder

sticky rice, to serve

Heat a heavy-bottomed cast-iron or grill pan over high heat. Pour a little vegetable oil onto a piece of paper towel and very carefully wipe the inside of the hot pan—if it smokes a little, that's great. Lift the steaks from the marinade and allow any excess marinade to drip into the bowl. Retain the marinade. Lay the steaks into the pan, leave exactly where they are for 1 minute, then turn them 45 degrees and cook for another minute. Flip the steaks over and repeat. They should be charred and dark on the outside and very rare on the inside. Transfer to a plate and leave somewhere warm to rest for about 8 minutes.

Meanwhile, heat a wok over high heat and add the sesame oil. Swirl the oil around and then toss in the broccoli, sugar snap peas, and pepper. Stir-fry for 2 minutes, then toss in the snow peas and scallions. Toss for 1 minute and throw in the lettuce, cilantro, green chiles, garlic, ginger, green peppercorns, and star anise. Stir-fry for 30 seconds, ensuring everything is well mixed. Drizzle a little of the retained marinade into the wok—it should sizzle and sear. Toss with the vegetables, then remove from the heat.

Working quickly, slice the steaks into thin strips and toss into the wok along with any escaping juice. Tip everything into a bowl, grab the sticky rice, and head toward the table.

PEPPERCORNS

You could write a book about pepper... hang on, several people have (I just checked), so I'll keep this short and cooklike. Black, white, and green peppercorns are all berries of a creeping vine. White peppercorns are harvested then soaked and dried to obtain the white seed. Chefs tend to use white peppercorns in their peppermills simply because it's less visible in sauces. Black peppercorns are also dried. My peppermill at home has black peppercorns in it because I prefer the more pungent kick they give. Green peppercorns appear a couple of times in this book. I am lucky to live close to a fabulous spice market where I can buy fresh green peppercorns on the vine. If you don't live near me, you could use a can of green peppercorns in brine to almost the same effect.

HOW TO MILK A COCONUT

If you came to cook in my restaurant, you would need a big glass of water every now and then to counteract the heat in the kitchen. Water in my part of the world is supplied free via a faucet, so I'd let you have as much as you wanted. In some parts of the world, free clean water is not such a basic provision, and so solutions are required. When I worked in Sri Lanka, the solution was coconuts! There was a cold room with a huge pile of green coconuts. You'd select one, lop off the top, stick a straw in, and drink the cold liquid inside, and here's my point—that liquid was not coconut milk. It was coconut water. Coconut milk is made by pouring boiling water over grated coconut flesh. I just wanted to clear that up!

I love coconut milk as a stock for cooking meat, vegetables, and seafood. If you were to cook every dish in this book, you would need to purchase a lot of the stuff, so it's worth discussing its availability. Most supermarkets sell coconut milk in cans. These are great and because they're widely available, I've used cans (on your behalf) in my recipe experiments (with complete success, by the way). When buying cans of coconut milk, check to ensure they are unsweetened, as supermarkets also sell that awful sugary coconut milk that bartenders like to pour into cocktails.

Coconut milk can be made from dried coconut, but I don't think the flavor or consistency is great. A much better option is to buy bags of frozen grated coconut to which you can add water, or simply add it into whatever you're cooking.

And then there is powdered coconut, to which one adds boiling water. This works much better than dried coconut because the flavor is good, and because it's made from a powder you get a better consistency.

Finally, a couple of recipes call for coconut cream. Coconut cream is made in exactly the same way as coconut milk, just with much less water. Coconut cream is great for desserts and enriching sauces. Again, avoid the sugary stuff loved by those pesky bartenders, and go instead for the natural unsweetened option.

I often struggle to find a suitable finale to a spicy meal. Fruit always works because it's so refreshing, but what if you want to impress? So developing the recipes in this chapter has really been an exercise in self-help!

Sweet, sweet spice

Okay, so we all know that panna cotta is an Italian dessert, and we may also know that, in Italy, coconut and lemongrass farming is a cottage industry at best. But I didn't know what else to call this dish, so as it follows the principles of Italian panna cotta production, panna cotta it is!

The pineapple and chile part may seem a bit wacky at first, but I'm not the first cook to use this combination in a dessert. Just trust me—it works. You'll note from the photograph that I serve my panna cottas in recycled jam jars, which makes me a modern, planet-friendly type of guy, and also saves a few bucks on fancy dishes. I'll let you decide which one was my motivation. A 'soft' dessert like this needs a bit of crunch, so I recommend Orange & Poppy Seed Snaps (see page 172) as the perfect solution. 99

Coconut & lemongrass panna cotta with sweet chile pineapple

MAKES ENOUGH FOR 6 SERVINGS (6 JAM JARS, THREE-QUARTERS FILLED)

3 sheets of gelatin

1⅔ cups coconut milk

1⅓ cups coconut cream

4 lemongrass stalks

½ cup sugar

grated zest and juice of 1 lime

4 tablespoons Greek yogurt

FOR THE SWEET CHILE PINEAPPLE

¾ cup pineapple juice

⅔ cup sugar

1 red chile, seeded, membrane removed, and very finely diced

½ pineapple, cut into ½-inch cubes

Lay the gelatin sheets flat on a plate and cover them with cold water. Leave to soak until they turn jellylike in consistency. Set aside.

Pour the coconut milk and coconut cream into a pan. Bash the lemongrass, a stalk at a time, using a rolling pin, until it splinters into shards. Add to the pan and push below the surface of the liquid. Add the sugar and lime zest and juice and heat to a simmer. Cook for 3 minutes, remove from the heat, and leave to stand for 5 minutes.

Pass the mixture through a fine sieve, making sure you push through all the liquid. Discard the stuff in the sieve. You now have a coconut-flavored liquid, lightly sweetened and infused with lime and lemongrass.

Squeeze the water from the gelatin and add to the hot liquid. Stir until the gelatin dissolves. Allow the mixture to cool a little and then gently whisk in the yogurt. Pour into 6 jars and chill in the fridge for 2 hours or until set.

Remove the panna cotta from the fridge about an hour before serving to allow to soften very slightly. Also, the flavor is better if they are not eaten straight from the fridge.

Meanwhile, make the sweet chile pineapple. Pour the pineapple juice into a small pan and stir in the sugar. Heat to a simmer and cook until reduced by a third to form an intense pineapple syrup. Remove from the heat and stir in the chile and pineapple. Chill in the fridge until required.

Spoon the chile pineapple over the coconut panna cotta, adding a little of the pineapple syrup as well.

At first glance, this dessert may look a little complicated, but ignore all the fancy-pants stuff around the outside—I will give you all the details for that in the recipe, but the main part of the dish is the creamy, frozen semifreddo under the glazed fig.

A semifreddo is a rustic-style Italian ice cream, which is perfect to make at home because all you need is a freezer rather than an expensive ice-cream machine.

I have flavored the semifreddo with two very pungent spices—cardamom and star anise—which go well with the honey, giving the dessert a Middle Eastern feel. Fig is the ideal fruit for this, although you could use poached plums or blackberries if figs aren't your thing.

Once you've mastered this recipe, you will be free to wander unaccompanied in the land of semifreddos, creating whatever combinations you wish by using the basic mixture and adding your chosen flavorings. Semifreddo is often made in a terrine mold and cut at the table. I prefer to use individual metal rings, but the choice is yours. I suggest making semifreddo at least a day before you need it so that it has time to freeze and set. You could, of course, make it days before and leave it in the freezer. If you're feeling really adventurous, or you need to impress your dinner guests, make the basil syrup, too. The flavor and color are stunning and it goes so well with this dessert, but the semifreddo still tastes great without it. ❞

Honey, cardamom & star anise semifreddo with roasted fig sauce & basil syrup

MAKES ENOUGH TO FILL 8 X 3-INCH RINGS

2 green cardamom pods

1 star anise

1 free-range egg, plus 4 yolks

⅓ cup honey

1¼ cups heavy cream

The first job is to grind the spices—without a doubt, this is best done minutes before using them so that their full, fresh pungency goes into the dessert. Grind the cardamom pods using a mortar and pestle. Give each a thud and you will see the pods splits open. Inside the green husks are some shiny, black seeds. Separate the seeds and discard the husks. Now add the star anise to the cardamom seeds and grind everything to a really fine powder.

To make the sabayon (see page 152) , put the egg, egg yolks, honey, and ground spices into a bowl set over a pan of simmering water and whisk for 5–6 minutes or until the mixture is pale, thick, and creamy (a steady whisking that incorporates all the mixture is much more effective than mad, crazy whisking that leaves you exhausted after 2 minutes!). Remove

MORE INGREDIENTS OVERLEAF ...

CONTINUED... ⟶

Honey, cardamom & star anise semifreddo with roasted fig sauce & basil syrup

CONTINUED FROM PAGE 151

FOR THE FIG SAUCE

3 figs

1 tablespoon sugar

3 tablespoons water

FOR THE BASIL SYRUP

½ cup water

1 cup sugar

small bunch of basil

FOR THE GLAZED FIGS

8 figs

confectioner's sugar, for dusting

TO SERVE

honey

8 teaspoons pine nuts (1 teaspoon
    for each person)

the bowl and continue whisking for around 5 minutes or until the mixture cools. Whip the cream until thickened but still loose enough that it will just about pour. Add the cream to the sabayon and carefully fold in.

Place 8 x 3-inch metal rings onto a lined baking sheet. Spoon the mixture into the rings and carefully slide the baking sheet into the freezer for 4 hours. Don't touch until you're ready to serve.

Now for the other things ...

To make the fig sauce, halve the figs, scrape out the flesh, and roughly chop. Transfer to a pan with the sugar and water. Heat to a simmer and cook for 5 minutes, then blend to a smooth sauce using an immersion blender.

To make the basil syrup, heat the water and sugar to a simmer and cook for 5 minutes. Meanwhile, process the basil in a blender or food processor. Pour the hot, simmering water and simple syrup onto the basil while the motor is at full speed and process until the basil is completely blended in. Strain to remove any bits and chill in the fridge until required.

The fig on top to serve is very easy. Halve the figs, dust the cut faces with confectioner's sugar and place under a hot broiler, or use a blowtorch to glaze (the figs don't need to be warm, so you can do this an hour or two in advance). Toast the pine nuts in the oven or a hot pan until golden brown.

Push the semifreddos out of the rings on to serving plates and place the glazed fig halves on top. Drizzle with a little honey, spoon around the fig sauce and basil syrup, and top with a few toasted pine nuts.

A WORD ON DESSERT JARGON

1. The process used to make the semifreddo has a fancy French name—you're making a *sabayon* from the eggs, the heat and the air that you're incorporating via the whisk. Expect the mixture to become pale in color, thick, and viscous. Bear in mind that if you neglect any area of the bowl, the egg in that part will cook firm from the heat of the bowl—your mission is to avoid this.

2. Chefs often tell people to "fold carefully." What we mean is to gently turn two whisked, aerated mixtures together so that the air is retained within, rather than knocking it out by vigorously stirring.

VANILLA

Because of my childhood introduction to vanilla via ice cream, I grew up thinking vanilla basically meant plain, as in no added flavor. How wrong was that? Vanilla is a big hitter in the flavor stakes. If you are ever lucky enough to visit a spice garden, you will be amazed to see vanilla growing on a vine from which long, green pods hang. If you are thinking of purchasing vanilla for one of the many (delightful, inspired, and tasty) recipes in this book, here are a couple of pointers.

Fresh vanilla is definitely the best. Well, I say fresh—it's actually steamed and fermented over several weeks before the cook lays hands upon it, but it's the real thing. The vanilla pod should be split and the seeds within scraped out, but whenever possible use both the pod and the scraped seeds because combined they impart the full flavor of vanilla. The flavor is also enhanced by being added to a fatty liquid such as cream, butter, or milk, which is why it works so well in ice creams.

Then there is vanilla extract. Not as good as the real thing, but useable nonetheless, and easy to use, too, as it arrives in a bottle. Finally comes the villain of the piece, vanilla essence. This really isn't anywhere near as good as either of the aforementioned vanillas—go without while you save up to treat yourself to the real thing!

By the way, scraped vanilla pods that haven't been cooked can be stored in a jar of sugar. The sugar will absorb much of the flavor.

" If my mother comes across this recipe, she will very probably threaten me with legal action, claiming that I've ripped off her famous banana and sour cream dessert without prior agreement. Mrs. Merrett does indeed make a very good banana and sour cream dessert, but I think I've taken the dish to new heights with my customization. The talking point in her dish is undoubtedly the melted caramel sugar topping, which I've kept here. But seriously Mom, mango and pineapple are so much more exciting than the overripe bananas you use, and everyone likes Greek yogurt more than sour cream.

The rice pudding is an element of the dish rather than the main focus, so don't be tempted to cook too much rice. I always use Carolina pudding rice for this because it's the standard rice recommended for a sweet rice pudding, but we recently forgot to order said rice at the restaurant and so my man on the pastry used risotto rice with equally good results. I recommend assembling this dessert about 3 hours before serving. "

Coconut rice pudding, fresh mango & pineapple with spiced brown sugar yogurt

SERVES 4

2 tablespoons butter

2½ tablespoons granulated or vanilla sugar (see page 153)

2 green cardamom pods

2 cloves

pinch of ground ginger

⅓ cup Carolina (see note in intro) or carnaroli rice

14oz can coconut milk

½ cup water

⅔ cup coconut cream

FOR THE SPICED BROWN SUGAR

½ cup dark brown sugar

½ teaspoon pumpkin pie spice

½ teaspoon ground cinnamon

TO SERVE

1 ripe mango, peeled, pitted, and cut into small cubes

chunk of ripe sweet pineapple, cut into small cubes

½ cup Greek yogurt

Melt the butter in a small pan over low heat. Add the sugar and the cardamom, cloves, and ginger. Let everything fizzle for a few seconds (I should explain that in my book—literally—fizzle happens at a lower heat than sizzle!). Add the rice and fizzle again for 1 minute.

Whisk together the coconut milk and the water (this will help the rice to absorb the liquid). Pour about ½ cup of the thinned coconut milk into the rice and stir to a simmer. Add the remaining thinned coconut milk a little at a time, bringing each addition to a simmer before adding more, stirring occasionally. By the time you've used up all the thinned coconut milk, the rice should be soft and edible with a coconut flavor and a little spicy zing. Remove from the heat and leave to cool for 10 minutes.

Stir in the coconut cream and leave to cool completely. Remove the cardamom pods and cloves, which should be fairly easy to find in the white rice pudding.

Meanwhile, stir together the ingredients for the spiced brown sugar.

About 3 hours ahead of serving, evenly distribute the mango among four jars or serving bowls. Spoon a layer of rice pudding over the mango, then add the pineapple and top with the yogurt. Sprinkle with the spiced brown sugar and cover (either with lids or plastic wrap) and leave in the fridge for 2 hours. The sugar will "melt" into the yogurt to make a lovely caramel topping…and annoy my mother.

" A short while ago, I received a phone call while at work. I didn't recognize the number, so I answered with an irritable snarl, presuming it would be one of those annoying calls from a call center, trying to sell me something I didn't need.

'Is that Mr. Paul Merrett?'

'Possibly... who is this? I'm extremely busy at the moment.'

'Oh, I am sorry. I represent a five-star luxury resort in the Maldives and we were wondering if you would consider coming out here, free of charge, with your family, as part of our guest chef promotion... I could call back.'

'Uh, no, actually I'm no longer busy in any way... I'll have to consider it, obviously.'

I turned away, covered the phone, and punched the air.

'Right, I've considered it—we're coming. Name the date.'

And so this dessert was born...

You don't have to eat it on a tropical island surrounded by powdery white sand and coral reef, though frankly it will taste a lot better if you do (as with every other recipe in this book!). A glance at the photo may put you off making it initially because it looks quite fancy, but I assure you it is not very tricky at all.

The almond paste, called frangipane by us catering types, is a classic French preparation used in many desserts. I tend to make more than I need and then freeze the excess in lumps for later use. As far as puff pastry is concerned, you could make it from scratch... but life is too short. Just buy a decent brand.

And so to the ice cream. Ten minutes ago I posted a message on Twitter asking if I could presume that my future book readers would own an ice-cream machine. The answer was a unanimous no. So here's plan B—a trick I've tried at home, after seeing a much better chef than I do it on TV. "

Mango & almond tarts with yogurt & black pepper ice cream

MAKES 4 INDIVIDUAL TARTS

10oz puff pastry
flour, for dusting
2–3 just ripe mangoes

FOR THE ALMOND PASTE
9 tablespoons butter
1⅓ cups almond flour
1¼ cups sifted confectioner's sugar
⅔ cup sifted flour
3 small eggs

To make the almond paste, beat the butter using an electric mixer for about 5 minutes, or until pale and fluffy (if you are mixing by hand, this will take considerably longer). Add the almond flour, confectioner's sugar, and flour and beat for another 5 minutes to form a dry paste.

Crack the eggs into a bowl and break up with a fork. With the mixer at low speed, gradually add the eggs to the paste, beating after each addition, until well combined. Chill in the fridge for at least 1 hour before use.

CONTINUED... ⟶

Mango & almond tarts with yogurt & black pepper ice cream

CONTINUED FROM PAGE 157

To prepare the tart cases, cut the puff pastry into 4 even chunks. Dust the work surface with flour and roll out a chunk quite thinly, then cut it into a disk about 5 inches across (I use a salad plate as a template). Prick the pastry disk with a fork and lay on a baking sheet lined with parchment paper. Rest the pastry in the fridge and repeat with the remaining 3 chunks.

Cutting the mangoes is the easiest part of the whole recipe, but the hardest for me to describe. Peel each mango carefully and slice off the "cheeks" from either side of the stone. Cut into flat, thin, half-moon-shaped slices.

Remove the puff pastry disks from the fridge and spread 2 tablespoons of almond paste onto each one to cover evenly. Place a slice of mango on top of the almond paste, ensuring the tips of the half moon are at the center and the outside edge of the disk. Arrange a second mango slice on top of the first to leave a small margin of the first mango slice still visible. Continue like this until you have gone all around.

About 1 hour before serving, preheat the oven to 325°F and bake the tarts for 15 minutes or until the undersides are golden brown. The tarts are nicest served at Maldivian room temperature, so set aside to cool a little before serving. Serve with the ice cream.

Yogurt & black pepper ice cream

SERVES 4

4 tablespoons Greek yogurt
1 tablespoon cracked black pepper
2 cups vanilla ice cream

This needs to be prepared well in advance.

Mix the yogurt with the black pepper at least an hour ahead of time and chill in the fridge. Also, put a metal or glass bowl in the fridge so that it's nice and cold.

Remove the ice cream from its container and place on a very clean cutting board. Keep the container handy. Quickly cut the ice cream into chunks and throw it into the cold bowl. Add the yogurt to the bowl and cut and mix the yogurt and ice cream together using a tablespoon. The whole operation should only take about 2 minutes.

Squelch the ice cream back into the container and put back in the freezer for at least an hour before serving.

66 I was incredibly lucky to spend time working in Sri Lanka, a country where the cuisine is very much a part of the rich cultural heritage. When I climbed off the plane, I thought a banana was, well, a banana. Back in England, I used to pick up the phone and ask for bananas and think nothing more of it. I soon realized that there are various types. In Sri Lanka, red bananas went in the hotel fruit bowls, the large starchy bananas were used in savory dishes, and the short, stubby, sweet bananas were for desserts. I have since seen these short, stubby bananas in supermarkets, so if you can get them for this dessert then great, since they are an ideal portion size—if not, I would go with a larger banana and cut it into two portions.

The syrup in which the bananas are poached is a big part of the dish. Be brave with the coffee, cardamom, and star anise—they are all very strong when eaten, but here they are simply used to infuse flavor. The bananas should be poached and cooled up to 4 hours in advance. I haven't included a brioche recipe since I'm presuming you're happy to buy some, or you have a good breadmaking book. 99

Poached bananas on toasted brioche with coffee bean, cardamom & star anise syrup

SERVES 4

3¾ cups water

1½ cups sugar

15 green cardamom pods, lightly crushed

1 cinnamon stick

10 star anise

6 tablespoons coffee beans

4 short, stubby bananas, sometimes called finger bananas

4 slices of brioche

good-quality vanilla ice cream, to serve

Pour the water into a pan and add the sugar, cardamom, cinnamon, star anise, and coffee beans. Bring to a simmer and cook for 20 minutes or until reduced by about half. Pass the spiced stock through a sieve and discard the spices and coffee beans. Pour back into the pan, return to the heat, and bring to a very gentle simmer.

Peel the bananas and drop them into the pan. Poach the bananas for around 3 minutes—they will swell and soften very slightly; the cooking time will depend a little on how ripe they are. Remove the pan from the heat and leave to cool for up to 4 hours.

To serve, pour 8 tablespoons of the banana syrup into a frying pan and bring to a boil (as the syrup boils it will reduce and thicken slightly). Place the bananas into the pan to warm, turning them to coat with the syrup.

Meanwhile, toast the brioche and place into four serving bowls. Put the warm bananas onto the brioche, top each serving with a scoop of ice cream, and drizzle on a little of the spiced syrup.

Tamarind trees grow throughout the tropical regions of the world, and the pods produced by the tree are an essential ingredient in local kitchens. Inside a tamarind pod is a gooey, dark pulp, which surrounds a bean or pit. The pulp is often used as an acidifying agent in dressings, marinades, chutneys, relishes, and many other dishes besides. Tamarind comes in various forms. The whole pods, which are used here, can be purchased from Asian supermarkets. Sometimes a tamarind cake is sold, which is basically the pulp, removed and pressed into a lump.

While tamarind is essentially sour, it is sometimes mixed with sugar and made into syrup for use in drinks and desserts. This is one such dessert. The dark, rich taste of the tamarind balances perfectly with the sweet custard. Think Asian-style crème brûlée and you won't be too far off the mark, but instead of a glazed sugar topping, this one has a terribly trendy, salted caramel praline crunch. The peanut crunch can be made a day or so in advance, then simply blended on the day.

Sweet tamarind custard with salted peanut crunch

SERVES 6

7oz tamarind pods
¾ cup full-fat milk
1 cup heavy cream
2 large eggs, plus 2 yolks
2 heaping teaspoons sugar
½ teaspoon ground cinnamon
freshly grated nutmeg

FOR THE SALTED PEANUT CRUNCH
1 cup sugar
3 tablespoons water
¾ cup salted peanuts
large pinch of sea salt flakes

First make the custard. Crack open the tamarind pods and remove the pulp. Soak the pulp in hot water for 10 minutes. Pick out the seeds from the soaked pulp and discard.

Preheat the oven to 250°F and line a 10-inch square baking dish with parchment paper. Bring the milk and cream to a simmer and add the tamarind pulp while gently whisking to combine.

Whisk the eggs, egg yolks, sugar and cinnamon together in a bowl. Pour the hot milk and cream into the egg mixture and leave to stand for 10 minutes.

Strain the mixture into a pitcher, using a spoon to push through any lumps of tamarind. Pour the custard into six ramekins (or you could use a large baking dish). Grate a little nutmeg over each of the custards.

Stand the ramekins in a roasting pan and pour boiling water around the ramekins so that it comes about halfway up the sides. Bake in the oven for 35 minutes or until the custards still have a definite wobble but feel loosely set to the touch. Leave to cool.

To make the salted peanut crunch, put the sugar into a small pan and slowly trickle in the water. Use a spoon to slowly turn the mixture until the sugar has dissolved.

Heat the pan over medium heat. Don't stir—let the mixture bubble until it forms a rich golden-brown caramel. Add the peanuts, remove from heat, and pour onto the lined baking sheet. Leave to cool completely.

Break up the (what is now called) praline, add the sea salt, and blend to a coarse crumb in a food processor. (Don't over-process—the peanut crunch needs a little texture.) Sprinkle on the custards just before serving.

> When I was about 14, my mother took us on our very first vacation abroad, to Spain. It left a massive impression on me for three reasons:
>
> 1. There were topless women on the beach.
>
> 2. My sister and I could electrocute each other by shuffling our feet along the hotel's synthetic carpet.
>
> 3. There was a van in the town that sold these long, thin, crispy things that tasted divine.
>
> All these years later I still love topless women...NO, that's wrong...I still love those crispy things that I now know are called 'churros.'
>
> If you've ever made choux pastry, you will notice distinct similarities between its and the churros' preparation. The mixture is simple to make and once you've piped out the churros you can freeze them, enabling you to have a crispy churros snack with a 'café con leche' at any time you wish. The churros we had in Spain were doused in either chocolate or caramel sauce, which as a kid I loved, but now I think that makes them far too sweet, and I prefer to serve them with a fruit fool. A fool is a purée of any fruit mixed with crème Anglaise and yogurt. You can make your own custard if you like, but a good store-bought one is fine, too.

Crispy sugar-spiced churros with blackberry yogurt fool

MAKES ABOUT 20 CHURROS, WHICH, FRANKLY, WILL NOT BE ENOUGH!

1¼ cups water

5 tablespoons vegetable oil,
   plus 2 cups for frying

1⅔ cups all-purpose flour

good pinch of salt

1 large egg, lightly beaten

1 cup sugar

1 tablespoon ground cinnamon

FOR THE BLACKBERRY YOGURT FOOL

1 cup blackberries

2 tablespoons sugar

½ cup Greek yogurt

½ cup cold custard or heavy cream

Pour the water and the 5 tablespoons oil into a large pan and bring to a boil.

Immediately tip in the flour and salt and stir with a wooden spoon for 5 minutes or until the mixture forms a dough that comes away from the edge of the pan cleanly. Don't allow the mixture to catch or it will burn. Transfer the dough to a bowl or the bowl of an electric mixer, if you have one, and leave to cool for about 15 minutes—a good time to make the fool.

For the fool, place the blackberries into a pan with the 2 tablespoons sugar and heat to a simmer. Cook for 3 minutes, then blend to a purée using an immersion blender. Strain to remove any seeds and leave to cool.

Return to the dough. Add the egg to the dough a little at a time, beating well after each addition. (It's easiest to do this using the beater attachment of an electric mixer, but if you do it by hand you will be burning calories, which you can then replace via churros consumption. Every cloud and all that!)

Spoon the dough into a piping bag with a largish, star-shaped nozzle attached, and pipe short sticks about 4 inches long onto parchment paper. The churros can either be frozen or cooked immediately. Mix the sugar with the cinnamon ready to coat the freshly cooked churros and set aside.

Pour the remaining vegetable oil into a large, heavy-bottomed pan and heat to 350°F. Carefully drop the churros into the oil (you can drop them in on the parchment paper if it's easier, since it will come away in the oil). Cook until golden all over, then carefully remove from the oil using a slotted spoon. Drain on paper towels and toss in the cinnamon sugar.

Mix in the yogurt and custard or cream with the cooled purée. Serve in a shot glass so the churros can be dipped in.

The recipe for Mango & Almond Tart with Yogurt & Black Pepper Ice Cream (see page 157) includes quantities for making more almond paste than required, and I noted in the introduction that the surplus could be used in other desserts. So, here is one such dessert. I'm including the recipe for the paste here as well, in case you haven't gotten around to trying my Mango & Almond Tart yet. The paste can be made a day or two in advance and kept in the fridge, or well in advance and frozen until required.

At the restaurant we serve these wontons as part of a bigger, more glamorous dessert, but I think they are great served simply with a scoop of ice cream. Wonton wrappers can be bought, usually frozen, from Asian supermarkets.

Almond, cinnamon & cranberry wontons

SERVES 4

⅓ cup dried cranberries, soaked in hot water for 10 minutes, then squeezed dry

½ teaspoon ground cinnamon

8 wonton wrappers, about 3 inches square

1 egg, beaten

1⅔ cups vegetable oil

confectioner's sugar, for dusting

4 scoops of your favorite vanilla ice cream, to serve

FOR THE ALMOND PASTE

9 tablespoons butter

1⅓ cups almond flour

1¼ cups sifted confectioner's sugar

⅔ cup sifted flour

3 small eggs

If you have already made the almond paste, skip this part. If not, read on. Beat the butter using an electric mixer for about 5 minutes or until pale and fluffy (if you are mixing by hand, this will take considerably longer). Tip in the almond flour, confectioner's sugar, and flour and beat for another 5 minutes to form a dry paste.

Crack the eggs into a bowl and break up with a fork. With the mixer at low speed, gradually add the eggs to the paste, beating after each addition until well combined. Chill in the fridge for at least 1 hour before use. Measure 6 ounces of the paste to use for the wontons and freeze the remainder.

To make the wontons, place the almond paste into a bowl and mix in the cranberries and cinnamon. Lay a wonton wrapper on a clean surface and place a walnut-sized spoon of almond paste in the center of the wrapper. Lightly brush the edges of the wrapper with the beaten egg. Place a second wrapper over the almond paste and gently flatten it down a bit so that the 2 wrappers meet and the egg "glues" them together. (I think it's nice if you don't quite match up the wrappers, meaning the second one goes on at a slightly different angle, giving a star-like appearance.) Repeat to make 4 wontons in total. Store in the fridge on parchment paper until you are ready to cook.

Pour the oil into a large pan to a depth of at least 4 inches and heat to 340°F. Carefully place the wontons in the hot oil and fry for 5 minutes or until golden brown and crispy, turning them over occasionally. Dust with confectioner's sugar and serve with vanilla ice cream.

66 Just say we decided to fire a space capsule to Mars filled with things that represented all that's good about Britain and just say I was asked to fill up the capsule, then this dessert is going in.

Any steamed pudding is worth making, but I think this version, with bananas, crunchy pecans, and warm spice, is my favorite. I've included a few serving options because the cream versus ice cream debate rages on in my house. 99

Steamed spiced pecan & banana pudding

SERVES 4

12 tablespoons unsalted butter, diced, plus extra for greasing

1½ cups self-rising flour

¾ cup sugar

3 eggs

3 bananas—overripe browning ones from the fruit bowl are ideal

1 teaspoon ground cinnamon

1 teaspoon pumpkin pie spice

1 teaspoon ground ginger

¼ cup plain yogurt

⅓ cup roughly chopped pecans

maple syrup

TO SERVE (I CAN'T DECIDE WHICH IS BEST—PERHAPS SERVE ALL OF THEM!)

vanilla ice cream, sprinkled with freshly grated nutmeg

dulce de leche

heavy cream

The best thing to make this in is one of those plastic pudding molds. They hold about 5 cups, which is ideal for this recipe. Alternatively, use individual-sized pudding molds and reduce the overall cooking time to about an hour.

Put the butter, flour, sugar, and eggs in a bowl and beat well until smooth—I use a traditional electric mixer, with the beater attached, but you could do it by hand or use a food processor. Peel the bananas, slice, and add to the bowl. Add the spices, yogurt and pecans and beat for 2 more minutes until well combined.

Spoon the mixture into a greased pudding mold, ensuring the basin isn't more than three-quarters full, allowing space for the pudding to rise. Place a piece of greased foil loosely over the top and secure with string.

Place the basin into a large pan and pour boiling water around the basin so that it comes two-thirds of the way up the sides. Cover with a lid and steam the pudding for 1½ hours or until a metal skewer inserted into the center comes out clean, adding more boiling water to the pan if necessary.

Carefully turn the pudding out onto a serving plate and drizzle over (drizzle? Who am I trying to kid! Slosh over, more like) plenty of maple syrup and serve with any of the other suggested accompaniments.

" This recipe is dedicated to Mrs. Page, my first cooking teacher, and it is the first dish she ever taught me. I would have been about eight years old and, while I had already developed a love of eating, I probably hadn't been let loose in a kitchen before. I still have the blue notebook in which we wrote the recipes—if I'd known back then that I would steal one for my own cookbook, I might have worked on making my handwriting a little clearer. This isn't the only reason I've included this recipe. Many of the ingredients are truly exotic and the flavors tell the story of wealth and empire.

I've changed the recipe very slightly from the rather more austere 1970s version given to me by Mrs. Page. I use unsalted butter rather than lard to make the pastry, golden raisins in place of black ones, and I use a decadent brown sugar with the apples rather than the standard-issue granulated. "

Spiced apple pie

SERVES 4 WITH ENOUGH FOR SECONDS

6 large apples, peeled and cut into 1-inch cubes

½ cup golden raisins

¾ cup brown sugar

½ teaspoon pumpkin pie spice

½ teaspoon ground ginger

pinch of grated nutmeg

1 tablespoon ground cinnamon

16 tablespoons (2 sticks) unsalted butter, diced and softened, plus extra for greasing

3¼ cups all-purpose flour

1 cup sugar

4 egg yolks, plus 1 white

2 tablespoons milk, plus a little extra for brushing

cream, to serve

The first thing to do is make the filling for the pie. Heat the apples, golden raisins, brown sugar, pumpkin pie spice, ginger, nutmeg, and cinnamon in a pan until the apples are just softened but not mushy. Transfer the apple mixture to a bowl and leave to cool. If the apples have produced lots of liquid, strain the mixture to prevent the pastry from becoming soggy from excess moisture. It's a shame to waste the apple and spice liquid, so I suggest adding it to your cream before serving.

To make the pastry, place the softened butter into a bowl and sift in the flour. Add the sugar, 3 of the egg yolks, and the egg white. Mix to form a smooth dough by hand or machine, then wrap in plastic wrap and leave to rest in the fridge for 30 minutes.

Preheat the oven to 350°F. Roll out two-thirds of the pastry to a thickness of about ½ inch and use it to line a 10-inch greased loose-bottomed tart pan. Trim any excess pastry and fill the center of the pie with the cooled apple mixture.

Roll out the remaining pastry to make the pie lid. Brush a little milk, or water, around the pie rim and lay the pastry lid over the apples. I like to crimp the edges slightly to make sure the pastry is well sealed.

Mix the remaining egg yolk with the milk and brush all over the pie. Use a fork to scribe a few decorative lines on top, if you so wish, and bake the pie for 30–40 minutes or until the pastry is golden brown. Carefully remove the flan ring, slide the pie on to a plate, and serve with cream.

“ Compared to our French, Spanish and Italian friends, we are not as steeped in ancient culinary tradition as we would sometimes like to believe. However, there are certain food-related topics that cause great debate.

Years ago I worked on the larder section in Gary Rhodes' restaurant. The larder was the section nearest the phone and it was my job to answer it ('Hello. Kitchen. Paul speaking, how may I help you?'). In one of his books, Gary gave a recipe for Cornish pasties and I can't tell you how many irate Cornish women phoned up to complain about some small detail or another.

Bakewell tart is another case in point. I recently made what I thought was a fairly reasonable Bakewell tart on TV, only to receive lengthy emails reminding me that the real recipe is a pudding rather than a tart, and unless my family had genetic Bakewell connections extending at least four generations back, I should keep my phoney recipe to myself. Well, I might be in similar trouble here, but I'm prepared to run the risk, rather than deny you what I believe is a truly fabulous dessert. Or is it a cake? Quick, switch phone to silent and turn off the computer.

Parkin cake originates from Yorkshire. Or is it Lancashire? Okay, northern England, and from the several recipes I've tried the main ingredients appear to be oatmeal, molasses, and spices. A tip that comes up time and time again is to make your parkin well in advance—if left for 3 or 4 days the cake develops a sticky richness that, connoisseurs agree, improves the taste.

I'm suggesting here that you serve parkin warm as a dessert, with toffee sauce and cream. However, to avoid controversy I have to admit that traditionally it is served as a cake with a good strong cup of tea. ”

Parkin with toffee sauce & cream

SERVES 15

2¾ cups all-purpose flour

¾ cup self-rising flour

2 teaspoons baking soda

4 teaspoons ground ginger

4 teaspoons ground cinnamon

2 teaspoons salt

1½ cups oatmeal, ground

1¾ cups sugar

16 tablespoons (2 sticks) butter

⅔ cup molasses

4 tablespoons corn syrup

4 eggs

1¼ cups milk

TO SERVE

16oz jar dulce de leche

lots of whipped cream

Preheat the oven to 350°F and grease and line a 9-inch square cake pan or deep baking dish. Combine both flours, the baking soda, ginger, cinnamon, salt, oatmeal, and sugar in a mixing bowl and set aside.

Melt the butter in a small pan and add the molasses and corn syrup. Stir until warmed through, then pour into the bowl of dry ingredients.

Beat together the eggs and milk and pour into the bowl, giving everything a good stir to ensure it's all well mixed. Pour the mixture into the prepared pan, and bake in the oven for 1 hour, or until the cake is risen and dark golden brown—a skewer inserted into the center should come out clean.

Now the tricky part. Transfer the cake to a wire rack to cool, then to a plastic container, and place in a cupboard for 3–4 days. Ouch! The cupboard needs to be locked in my house.

To serve, cut a decent portion of parkin per person and warm it slightly either in the microwave or by gently heating in a low oven. Warm a little of the dulce de leche and pour over the parkin. Add a generous amount of whipped cream and reserve a spot on the sofa to sleep off the joy of parkin.

There will be a few readers somewhat surprised to learn that baklava did not originate sometime during the 1990s. It is, in fact, a sweet treat with roots stretching as far back as the Ottoman Empire, and has since been a staple sugary hit throughout the Middle East, the eastern Mediterranean and, of course, places closer to home. As a kid I can remember my mother talking about baklava—she had spent part of her youth in Nicosia, Cyprus, where baklava was enjoyed in coffee bars alongside strong bitter coffee.

Back in the 1970s, there weren't that many Middle Eastern confectioners knocking out baklava for the enjoyment of us locals, so my own baklava experience was put on hold until I signed up for my apprenticeship at The Ritz London. At the time many of the big spenders in London hotels were from the Middle East, so our pastry section made sure that baklava was available alongside the more traditional European cookies, cakes, and desserts.

I like to serve baklava as a dessert rather than as a sweet snack or treat, but this recipe can easily check both boxes. There are so many baklava recipes in existence that it makes pinpointing an original very difficult, and very slightly pointless because the vast majority taste fabulous anyway!

A quick word on phyllo dough—there are many brands available but not all work as well as others, so shop around until you find one that you like.

Pecan & walnut baklava with apricots, Greek yogurt & honey

SERVES 4–6

1¼ cups pecans

1¼ cups walnuts

1 teaspoon ground cinnamon

1 teaspoon pumpkin pie spice

3 tablespoons brown sugar

10 tablespoons unsalted butter

20 sheets ready-made phyllo dough

FOR THE SYRUP

¾ cup sugar

1 tablespoon lemon juice

1 tablespoon orange blossom water

½ cup water

TO SERVE

1 cup Greek yogurt

4 very ripe apricots, pitted and cut into wedges

2 tablespoons honey

Before you begin, find a suitable baking dish. The one I use is stainless steel (allowing for good heat transference, so the bottom of the baklava will cook easily), 8 x 12 inches and 3 inches deep. If yours is slightly smaller or larger, simply cut the phyllo sheets to fit. Preheat the oven to 350°F.

Chop the nuts in a food processor until they resemble coarse bread crumbs, tip into a bowl, and mix in the spices and sugar. Set aside.

Melt the butter in the microwave—it should be very soft but not split and oily. Brush the bottom of the baking dish with a little of the butter. Cut the phyllo sheets to the size of the baking tray. You will need 20 layers in total. Once you have cut the phyllo, keep it in the fridge, on a tray, covered with a cloth.

Lay a sheet of phyllo on the baking sheet and brush with melted butter. Lay another sheet of phyllo on top of the first and brush with butter, then repeat with 8 more sheets to form 10 layers.

Sprinkle the nuts evenly over the top layer of phyllo. Place a phyllo sheet on top of the nuts, brush with butter, and repeat with the remaining pastry, giving 20 layers of phyllo in total.

Using a very sharp knife, cut diagonal lines across the pastry almost down to the nut layer. Turn the baking dish and cut lines diagonal to the first to create a diamond pattern. Bake in the oven for 35 minutes or until golden, puffed up, and crispy. Leave to cool.

Meanwhile, make the syrup. Heat all the ingredients in a small pan to a simmer and cook until reduced by a third to form a thickish syrup. Pour the syrup over the baklava into the cuts in the pastry. Leave to stand for at least an hour or overnight, if possible, before attempting to cut the baklava.

To serve, cut the baklava into small slabs and serve with a blob of Greek yogurt, wedges of apricot, and a good trickle of honey.

I'm including this recipe, a twist on the classic brandy snap, because so many desserts need just a little crunch on the side to wrap them up. I've omitted the word 'brandy' from the title because I've omitted it from the ingredients! I can never taste the brandy in a brandy snap, so why not save the money?

You could make nice, round, flat snaps to serve with a dessert as a thin, crisp cookie. However, there are those who like to curl up their snaps into various shapes and designs—please feel free to be as artistic as you wish.

Orange & poppy seed snaps

MAKES 16 SMALL SNAPS, OR 8 LARGE ONES, OR 4 VERY LARGE ONES, OR 2 ENORMOUS ONES

7 tablespoons butter

½ cup sugar

4 tablespoons corn syrup

½ cup all-purpose flour

1 teaspoon ground ginger

1 teaspoon ground cinnamon

1 tablespoon poppy seeds

grated zest of 1 large orange

Heat the butter, sugar, and corn syrup in a small pan until melted and gently bubbling.

Stir in the remaining ingredients. Remove the pan from the heat, transfer the mixture to a small bowl, and leave to cool completely. At this stage you can chill the mixture in the fridge for later use. If your snaps are not required today, definitely chill the mixture, as they are best fresh.

When you are ready to cook the snaps, preheat the oven to 350°F. Roll the mixture into balls about the size of a large hazelnut (this will yield 16 round snaps, about 3 inches across) and place the balls on a nonstick baking sheet, leaving enough space between each one to allow them to spread and flatten out.

Bake in the oven for 5 minutes or until the snaps are a golden caramel color and lacy in appearance. At this point you could roll them around the handle of a wooden spoon... or allow to cool, then carefully remove the now-brittle snaps from the baking sheet using an offset spatula.

“ Until very recently, I thought my grandmother invented the Easter cookie. The whole family loved these spicy, buttery cookies packed with currants, cinnamon, pumpkin pie spice, and lemon. Being a traditionalist, Granny only ever made these at Easter, refusing our enthusiastic requests for a similar cookie at any other time of the year. It turns out that Easter cookies are traditionally cooked and served at the aforementioned religious holiday, but I can honestly say I've never been offered one by anybody, before or since, which is why I emailed my Dad, requesting what I believed to be Granny's very own self-written recipe.

After a lot of chat about poor health, bad weather, and economic hardship, the old guy finally dropped the following bombshell:

'Anyway, here's the recipe—taken from the *Radiation Cookery Book for use with the New World Regulo-Controlled Gas Cookers* (19th Edition, 1936). They don't give the temperatures for modern ovens, but you're the expert and should know. Good old Granny, it's nice that she's remembered, especially in print.'

Good old Granny indeed. The cunning old lady had me believing she invented everything she cooked, and never owned a recipe book! Anyway, family traumas aside, do try these at any time of year. They are fabulous. ”

Spiced Easter cookies

MAKES 10 COOKIES

1¾ cups all-purpose flour
8 tablespoons (1 stick) butter
½ cup sugar
good pinch of grated lemon zest
½ teaspoon baking powder
⅓ cup golden raisins
½ teaspoon pumpkin pie spice
½ teaspoon ground cinnamon
1 egg, beaten
confectioner's sugar, for dusting

Preheat the oven to 325°F. Tip the flour into a bowl and lightly rub in the butter until the mixture resembles fine bread crumbs. Add the sugar, lemon zest, baking powder, golden raisins, and spices. Add the egg and gently mix to form a dough.

Roll the dough out to a thickness of about ½ inch and cut into disks using a 3½ inch cookie cutter. Place the cookies on a lined baking sheet and bake in the oven for 15 minutes.

Sprinkle with confectioner's sugar as soon as they come out of the oven, leave to cool, and serve.

Summer berries, spiced phyllo wafers & mascarpone & vanilla cream

SERVES 4

4oz raspberries

4oz blueberries

4oz strawberries

FOR THE PHYLLO WAFERS

1 package of phyllo dough

7 tablespoons butter

4 tablespoons brown sugar

½ teaspoon pumpkin pie spice

½ teaspoon ground ginger

1 teaspoon ground cinnamon

FOR THE MASCARPONE & VANILLA CREAM

1 cup mascarpone

½ cup Greek yogurt

seeds from 2 vanilla pods

2½ tablespoons confectioner's sugar

FOR THE BERRY SAUCE

8oz mixed berries—overripe,
    past-their-best ones are ideal
    for this

¼ cup sugar

As with most recipes, this one is easier when broken down into stages.

The phyllo wafers can be made well in advance—a couple of days, as long as they are stored in an airtight container. All of my previous speeches on phyllo dough apply: shop around until you find a brand you like. Whichever brand you choose, phyllo should always be kept in the fridge when not being worked on. So, preheat your oven to 325°F, then soften the butter. Line a flat baking sheet with parchment paper.

Mix the brown sugar with the ground spices. Now cut 16 squares of phyllo to 3 x 3 inches each (this will make 8 wafers—giving each person 2 wafers). Place 14 of the squares in the fridge. Place one of the remaining squares on the baking sheet, brush all over with a little butter and sprinkle it liberally with the sugar and spice mix. Then place the second square of phyllo on top, very slightly offset. Brush the top of this square with butter and sprinkle once more with the sugar and spice mix. This is your wafer—ready for baking. Make another 7 of these with the remaining 14 squares. Just before cooking them, place the palm of your hand on top of each wafer and give them a good press. Place the baking sheet in the oven and bake for 5–6 minutes until they are golden brown all over. Allow them to cool.

The mascarpone and vanilla cream can be made a few hours in advance. Beat the mascarpone, yogurt, vanilla, and confectioner's sugar in a bowl with a wooden spoon. Done. Store in the fridge until required.

You can make the berry sauce (called "coulis" in the restaurant world) fresh each time or prepare a bigger batch and freeze it when berries are plentiful and cheap. Tip the berries (for the sauce) into a small saucepan and sprinkle in the sugar. Heat gently until they simmer. Allow them to simmer for 3 minutes and then blend to a sauce in a blender. If the sauce is very thick, add a little water to thin it. Chill the sauce before using.

When you are ready to serve, place a wafer on each person's plate and spoon the mascarpone and vanilla cream on top. Place the second wafer on top of the mascarpone cream and dust with a little confectioner's sugar. Mix the whole raspberries, blueberries, and strawberries with the berry sauce and spoon over and around the wafers.

This is the section that can turn a decent meal into a fabulous one. Pickles, relishes, jams, vegetable dishes and bread are all great additions to many of the previous dishes and, in fact, some, like Imam Bayildi, Sag Aloo, or Matar Paneer, could all count as a meal on their own.

A bit on the side

66 Most of the savory recipes in this book would go well with a slab of flatbread. You can, of course, buy flatbreads of various types from supermarkets and they're really quite good quality. If you decide to go down this route, it's worth knowing that all of the varieties will benefit from being reheated in a very hot, ridged grill pan, or better still, a barbecue, rather than the manufacturer's recommendation of a hot oven. But perhaps you bought this book because you're into cooking, in which case it's my duty to provide a "make your own bread" option. Breadmaking is a skill that even some chefs never master. This is borne out by the fact that so many restaurants buy in their bread rather than make their own. Flatbread is an excellent starting point for the novice baker because the process avoids difficult procedures such as shaping loaves and baking at precise temperatures. Once you have made your dough, it's basically good to go. 99

Flatbread

MAKES ABOUT 12 PIECES

8 cups all-purpose flour

3½ cups very slightly warm water

4½ teaspoons dried yeast

5 tablespoons olive oil

5 teaspoons salt

A USEFUL TIP

If all of the above feels like a daunting process to carry out while simultaneously having to cook the actual dinner, it's worth pointing out that the raw bread can be frozen. This means you could make it a day or so in advance. If this idea appeals, follow all the instructions up to the point where you have a stack of rolled-out raw flatbreads separated by parchment paper. Stick this stack in the freezer. On the day, take out as many flatbreads as are required and allow to thaw for about 30 minutes, then proceed to the cooking stage.

STAGE 1

One of the reasons people tend to forgo breadmaking is the time involved—this recipe is no different on that score, but with a bit of time management you will be able to work around this issue. The first stage is to activate the yeast. Mix 1⅔ cups of the flour with ⅔ cup of the warm water and all the dried yeast—mix it up by hand in a mixing bowl. Cover the bowl with plastic wrap and leave for 3 hours on your kitchen worktop, in which time the yeast will activate, develop, and start to rise. Three hours is a long time, but you don't need to sit and watch it. You could go out for a walk, catch up on some TV, or prepare the rest of your meal.

STAGE 2—WITH A MACHINE

Uncover the bowl. The dough inside will be bubbly in appearance and very slightly risen. Take this sticky dough and transfer it to the bowl of your electric mixer. Add the rest of the ingredients—the remaining flour and water, the olive oil, and the salt. Mix everything with a wooden spoon just to get it started and then attach the dough hook to your machine and start the motor running on medium speed. The dough hook is designed to work, stretch, and pull the dough—bakers would call this process "kneading." The dough will seem quite wet, but do not add any more flour. Keep mixing the dough until it comes together as a silky-textured ball of dough—this could take 10 minutes or so.

STAGE 2—BY HAND

Uncover the bowl. The dough inside will be bubbly in appearance and very slightly risen. Add the rest of the ingredients—the remaining flour and water, the olive oil and the salt. Mix everything with a wooden spoon just to get it started and then roll up your sleeve and, using your hand, work the mixture until it's thoroughly combined. Turn this (very sticky) mixture onto a clean work surface and form it into a ball. In one motion, push the palm

Your flatbread can be flavored in many ways. Here are a few:

Saffron flatbread—add a pinch of saffron to the water right at the beginning

Herb flatbread—add chopped cilantro, parsley, or rosemary to the dough at the mixing stage

Seed and spice flatbread—cumin, onion, fennel, or sesame seeds can all be added to the dough at the mixing stage

Coconut flatbread—replace 10 percent of the flour with the same amount of grated coconut and use the water inside the coconut in place of tap water

Whole-wheat flatbread—replace 60 percent of the all-purpose flour with whole-wheat flour

of your hand into the dough, pushing it forward and stretching the dough, then pull back your hand, forming a rough ball once more. Bakers would call this process "kneading." The dough will feel very sticky and you will be sorely tempted to add more flour to counteract this. But don't! Persevere … Eventually, the stickiness will recede and you will be left with a silky-smooth dough. By hand, this kneading process could take half an hour of strenuous work—leaving you plenty of time to ponder why you have never invested in an electric mixer!

STAGE 3

Put the silky ball of dough into a large, clean bowl and cover the top of the bowl with a clean cloth. Leave this on the side in your kitchen for about an hour, in which time the dough will almost double in size.

STAGE 4

Uncover the bowl and, using your fist, push the top of the dough gently back into itself in a couple of places. The dough will expel gas and recede in size. Bakers call this process "knocking back." Take the knocked-back dough out of the bowl—do this by sliding your hand down the side of the bowl and under the dough and then lifting the whole piece out in one. Place the dough on a clean surface and gently form it into a ball.

Using a sharp knife, cut the dough into 12–14 even pieces and gently shape each piece into a rough ball shape. Lightly dust the work surface with a little flour and roll out one of the balls until you have a thin disc. Roll out the remaining balls of dough in the same way. You could stack them up as you go by painting each side of the rolled-out dough with a little olive oil and then putting a piece of parchment paper on top before adding the next piece of rolled-out dough.

COOKING

Your rolled-out stack of flatbread is best stored in the fridge if you're not cooking it immediately. It will be fine for an hour or so. The very best results are achieved over hot coals—a barbecue is excellent for cooking flat bread. If it's midwinter and a barbecue is out of the question, a ridged grill pan is the next best thing. Either way, gently brush some olive oil onto the flatbread and lay it on the very hot bars. When it starts to get puffy, turn it over and cook the other side. A little charring is a good thing, adding to the overall flavor. Serve immediately.

66 Baba ghanoush is made from charred eggplant and is popular throughout the Middle East. There are as many recipes for it as there are claims for country of origin. My suggestion is to try several different recipes before coming back to this book and agreeing that the following one is actually the best! It's often served as part of a mezze plate, but I use it as an integral part of various dishes, including my Dhana Jeera Spiced Lamb Rump (see page 96). 99

Baba ghanoush

SERVES 8 AS A DIP

2 eggplants

¼ cup olive oil

1 tablespoon tahini

2 garlic cloves, mashed to a purée

juice of ¼ lemon

2 tablespoons Greek yogurt

½ teaspoon salt

good twist of pepper

Heat a grill pan over high heat until really hot. Prick the eggplants all over with a fork, lay them in the grill pan, and leave to cook for 10 minutes or until blackened. Turn the eggplants over and cook for another 10 minutes. Turn them on their sides and cook until charred and crispy all over (this may take up to 40 minutes in total). They may smell as if they are burning, but fear not—this is a good thing! The reason for charring the outside is to give the inside a smoky taste. The eggplants will collapse a little as they cook. Transfer to a bowl to cool, reserving any juice.

Cut each eggplant in half and use a spoon to scrape out all the flesh, right down to the charred skin. Place the flesh on a cutting board and chop to a coarse purée using a large knife. Transfer the purée back to the bowl with any reserved juice. Add the remaining ingredients, stir really well and serve.

66 I'm fairly sure most of you will have at least eaten this, if not made it in some form or another. Tzatziki is a great accompaniment to many hot and spicy dishes, so I thought I'd include my version here. Avoid using any yogurt calling itself Greek-style yogurt and instead go for the traditional strained Greek stuff—it's richer, thicker, and creamier. 99

Tzatziki

SERVES 4 AS AN APPETIZER WITH PITA BREAD, OR 6—8 AS A SIDE DISH

1 large cucumber, peeled, sliced in half lengthwise and seeded

1 teaspoon table salt

2 garlic cloves, finely chopped

squeeze of lemon juice

1½ cups Greek yogurt

1 tablespoon olive oil

½ teaspoon shredded mint leaves

½ teaspoon chopped dill

Grate the cucumber on the coarsest side of your grater—longer slivers are best, so grate it from top to bottom, right along the cucumber's length. Place the cucumber into a bowl, sprinkle on the salt, and stir: it will start to release its juice. Hang the cucumber in cheesecloth for about 20 minutes or simply squeeze it inside a clean towel to remove as much liquid as possible.

Return the strained cucumber to the bowl, mix in the remaining ingredients, and serve immediately.

The best mangoes for this job are green mangoes, which are fairly easy to find in Asian food stores; however, a slightly firmer standard mango will suffice. I serve this with Braised Pork Cheeks with Coconut & Lime Leaf (see page 89), but the "noodles" go equally well with crispy squid or a grilled spice-rubbed breast of chicken. I recommend making the pickling liquid 24 hours in advance, if possible, so that the flavors can mingle and develop. The pickling liquid works well with other vegetables, too. Try adding to shredded white cabbage, strips of cucumber, or even avocado.

Soured mango "noodles"

SERVES 4

2 tablespoons sesame oil

2 tablespoons white wine vinegar

3 tablespoons fish sauce

juice of 2 limes

2½ tablespoons sugar

1 red chile, finely chopped

½ cup peeled and finely grated galangal

2 green mangoes (but normal ripe yellow mangoes would be fine)

1 tablespoon black sesame seeds

Whisk together the sesame oil, white wine vinegar, fish sauce, and lime juice. Add the sugar, chile, and galangal, and chill in the fridge overnight. This is your pickling liquid.

Prepare and marinate the mangoes about an hour before you wish to serve them. Thinly slice the mango flesh and then shred the slices into noodle-like strips. Add the strips of mango to the pickling liquid and leave to stand for about 15 minutes.

Drain the mango "noodles" of any excess liquid, stir through the sesame seeds and serve.

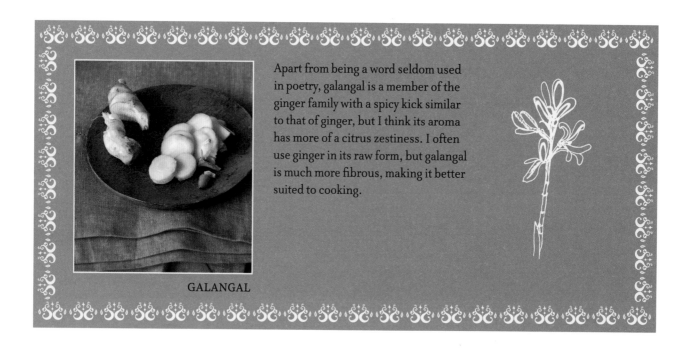

GALANGAL

Apart from being a word seldom used in poetry, galangal is a member of the ginger family with a spicy kick similar to that of ginger, but I think its aroma has more of a citrus zestiness. I often use ginger in its raw form, but galangal is much more fibrous, making it better suited to cooking.

> 66 Commonly used throughout Asian cooking, crispy shallots can be bought, already fried and crispy, in practically any Asian store, and to be honest most of the time that is exactly what I do. However, for readers living halfway up a mountain or on a desert island, or for the truly committed, here is how it's done. I often serve a bowl on the table for people to sprinkle on their food. 99

Crispy shallots

SERVES 8–10

9 banana shallots
4 cups vegetable oil

Peel the shallots and slice into thin rings (I use a mandoline for this but a sharp knife will do the job). Pour the vegetable oil into a deep-fryer or a pan large enough to allow for the oil to fizz during cooking. Heat the oil to 300°F and add the shallots. Stir continuously using a slotted spoon for 15 minutes or until the shallots are golden and crispy.

Carefully remove the shallots from the oil using the slotted spoon and lay them on a clean, dry towel. Leave to cool slightly, then fold the towel up and around the shallots and squeeze hard to remove excess oil.

Transfer the shallots to paper towels and spread them out to dry more. The above will give you Crispy Shallots but to improve the flavor, try this…

A SWEET AND SALTY CUSTOMIZATION—SHALLOT CRUNCH

This variation is used for the Shallot Crunch in the Salmon Sashimi recipe (see page 53). The quantities given here will provide plenty to top the sashimi.

One batch Crispy Shallots, bought or homemade
½ teaspoon salt
1 tablespoon sugar
pinch of red pepper flakes

Place all of the ingredients into a food processor and process to a fine crumb. Dip your finger in (I tend to stop the blade rotating first!) and taste. There should be a good, roasted Crispy Shallot taste as well as a spicy kick and an interesting sweet and salty flavor.

" Sambals are big news in Sri Lanka, where all curries are accompanied by a sambal of some variety, and this is my favorite. Serve a bowl of this on the table and let people add as much or as little as they like. My sambal can be served immediately or warmed slightly in the oven first.

Maldive fish flakes are widely used as seasoning in Sri Lanka as well as in the Maldives. They are made from tuna, which has been boiled, smoked, and dried to produce a woodlike chunk of fish. Frankly they stink, and when I first encountered them I thought only a crazy person would think that they would enhance food of any type, but I was wrong. They add a depth of flavor that salt alone cannot match. However, if you can't get them, do substitute salt. "

Coconut sambal

SERVES 4

1 coconut, halved

1 teaspoon black peppercorns

1 teaspoon paprika

1½ teaspoons chile powder

12 curry leaves

1 garlic clove, crushed

½ small red onion, finely chopped

1 tablespoon Maldive fish flakes, or 1 teaspoon salt

juice of 2 limes

Remove the flesh from the coconut halves and grate it using the finest side of a grater. Set the grated flesh aside and discard the shells.

Grind the peppercorns to a fine powder using a mortar and pestle and tip into a small mixing bowl, then add the paprika and chile powder. Grind the curry leaves, garlic, and red onion in the mortar and pestle and add to the bowl with the Maldive fish flakes or salt.

Add the coconut and lime juice and mix thoroughly. Serve to accompany curries.

" In his excellent book *The Oxford Companion to Food*, Alan Davidson informs us that the name "plantain" is given to any variety of banana which is suitable only for cooking. Furthermore he explains that, to the botanist, there is in fact no distinction at all between plantains and regular bananas. That's all well and good if you're a botanist, but we're not. We are cooks, and to you and me there is a huge difference. Bananas are short, bright yellow, and eaten raw when ripe, whereas plantains are harvested when under-ripe, while still green in fact, are very starchy, and therefore require cooking. They can be fried, baked, and grilled. I've had them curried in the Maldives, and as a porridge-like dish in East Africa, but we are going to make Plantain Chips, which are very easy, tasty ,and a good starting point for the plantain novice. "

Plantain chips

THIS WILL MAKE ENOUGH FOR 4 PEOPLE TO ENJOY AS A SNACK

1 plantain

1¼ cups vegetable oil

good pinch of sea salt flakes

Peel the plantain (this will not be as easy as peeling a banana and you may even resort to using a knife) and cut into thin slices using a sharp knife or a snazzy Japanese mandoline. Heat the vegetable oil in a pan until hot, but not smoking hot. Fry the slices in a couple of batches until golden and crispy (2–3 minutes). Carefully remove the chips using a slotted spoon, drain on paper towels, and sprinkle with the salt. I like to serve these with drinks before a spicy meal.

Asian cucumber pickle

MAKES ABOUT 20 SERVINGS

4 cucumbers, peeled and cut into thirds

$2/3$ cup vegetable oil

2 garlic cloves, finely chopped

2 red chiles, finely diced

5 tablespoons soy sauce

$1\frac{1}{2}$ tablespoons white wine vinegar

$2\frac{1}{2}$ tablespoons sugar

10 scallions, finely sliced on an angle

Grate the cucumbers using the coarsest side of a box grater. Run each cucumber chunk all the way along the grater to produce long, thin slivers until you reach the seeds, then turn the cucumber around and do the other side. Grate each chunk of cucumber until all you're left with are the seeds in the middle, then discard the seeds. Wrap the grated cucumber in a clean towel and squeeze really hard to expel as much moisture as possible. When you think you've got enough out, re-roll it and squeeze again, then set aside.

Heat the vegetable oil in a frying pan and gently cook the garlic and chiles for a minute or so (no browning is required, just a short fizz in the hot oil). Add the soy sauce, vinegar, and sugar and bring to a simmer. Add the cucumber and use a fork to loosen the strands within the hot liquid. Work quickly because you don't want to overcook it—3 minutes max!

Add the scallions, give everything a very quick stir, and remove from the heat. Leave the pickle to cool, then store in a sterilized jar in the fridge for up to 14 days.

Tomato chile jam

MAKES ENOUGH TO FILL 4 JAM JARS

3⅓ lbs ripe cherry tomatoes, halved

2 cups water

1¼ cups white wine vinegar

3¾ cups sugar

1 tablespoon yellow mustard seeds

1 tablespoon black mustard seeds

3 garlic cloves, finely chopped

2 heaping teaspoons red pepper flakes

Tip the cherry tomatoes into a saucepan. Add all the other ingredients to the pan, bring to a simmer, and cook for an hour or until the mixture takes on a thin, jammy appearance. Reduce the heat and cook until the jam thickens up a bit more, stirring occasionally to prevent it catching on the bottom.

Switch off the heat under the pan when you're happy with its appearance and carry out a jam test. Place a small spoon of the jam on a cold plate in your fridge. After a few minutes it will set to its final consistency. If you're happy with the consistency, great; if you think it's too thin, return to the heat for a few minutes.

Transfer to sterilized jars and store in the fridge for up to 2 months.

Sweet pepper relish

MAKES ENOUGH TO FILL 1 LARGE JAR

1 tablespoon olive oil

½ red onion, finely sliced

2 yellow peppers, finely sliced

2 red peppers, finely sliced

3 tablespoons pine nuts

20 pitted green olives, each sliced into 3 pieces crosswise

⅓ cup golden raisins

3 tablespoons red wine vinegar

5 tablespoons honey

6 tablespoons water

Heat the olive oil in a saucepan over high heat and tip in the red onions. Allow them to sizzle away for 1 minute. Add all the peppers and let sizzle for 5–6 minutes—the peppers should begin to soften slightly. Add the pine nuts, olives, and golden raisins, and give it a stir. Pour in the red wine vinegar, honey, and the water. Allow all this to simmer rapidly, stirring every now and then and making sure everything is pushed flat in the pan to benefit from the heat of the liquid. The peppers will by now have softened completely. When the liquid has reduced almost totally, your relish is done—about 8 minutes.

Remove the pan from the heat and cool completely before spooning the relish into a sterilized jar. The relish will improve and develop in flavor if left for a couple of days and will last up to 2 weeks if kept tightly closed.

Mango & red pepper jam

MAKES 1 JAR

splash of vegetable oil

1 red onion, cut into small dice

1 red pepper, cut into small dice

½ teaspoon red pepper flakes

6oz mango chutney (shh!)

1 large, ripe mango, peeled and cut into small dice

Heat a small pan, literally wet the bottom with some vegetable oil, and quickly cook the onion and pepper for 2 minutes until the onion is translucent but not colored. Sprinkle in the red pepper flakes and add the mango chutney. Stir and heat through, then add the mango. Simmer for 2 minutes, then remove from the heat and allow to cool completely.

Transfer to a sterilized jar, label "homemade," and keep quiet about the ready-made mango chutney maneuver! It should store in the fridge for up to 2 weeks.

Mint & mango yogurt dip

MAKES 500ML

5 tablespoons of your favorite store-bought mango chutney

2 tablespoons jarred mint sauce

1⅔ cups Greek yogurt

My favorite jarred mango chutney has large pieces of mango in it (and that's why it's my favorite). If yours does, too, you may want to chop the mango up a bit before adding it to the dip. Then all you need to do is mix all the ingredients together and stick it in the fridge until required.

Green tomato salsa

SERVES 4

1 lb green tomatoes, finely chopped

20 mint leaves, shredded

juice of 2 limes

2–4 green bird's eye chiles, finely chopped

4 scallions, very finely sliced

3 tablespoons finely shredded cilantro

1 tablespoon sugar

1 cup extra virgin olive oil

Mix all the ingredients together in a small bowl, adding the chiles to taste, and leave to stand at room temperature for 1 hour.

Spoon over whatever appeals to you.

A stupidly simple dip

SERVES ENOUGH FOR 4 WITH THE SHRIMP SESAME TOAST (PAGE 55)

4 tablespoons dark soy sauce

½ tablespoon sesame oil

1 tablespoon sweet chile sauce

2 garlic cloves, very finely chopped

½ teaspoon red pepper flakes

Mix it all up and get dipping!

This dish was invented in a West London gastro pub in 1995 and shortly afterwards the UK government passed a law enforcing every gastro pub chef in the country to cook a version of the dish and have it available on their menu at all times... or so it seemed.

Imam Bayildi is actually a Turkish dish, literally meaning "the imam (priest) fainted," and everyone already knows that fact because, in the late 90s, the UK government passed a second law insisting that every gastro pub chef should, at some time, show up on TV cooking said dish.

(Umm, yes, I did cook it on TV once...)

What I'm suggesting is that Imam Bayildi became a real gastro-pub favorite, but not without good cause. It's a fabulously spicy, evocative dish that can be eaten on its own or as an accompaniment to lamb or chicken. There are as many versions of the recipe as there are gastro pubs in London, and each one claims to be the original and the best. Here is my version, which I think you will find is the original and the best.

Imam bayildi

SERVES 6 AS AN ACCOMPANIMENT

2 cups olive oil

2 large eggplants, cut into large dice

1 large onion, finely diced

4 garlic cloves, chopped

1 teaspoon ground cinnamon (definitely best freshly ground from whole sticks)

1 teaspoon cumin seeds, toasted and ground

1 teaspoon ground allspice

1 teaspoon red pepper flakes

1 clove, ground

14 oz can chopped tomatoes (you can, of course, use fresh tomatoes if you wish—I was just keeping it simple)

2 tablespoons golden raisins

large pinch of salt

1 tablespoon chopped mint

2 tablespoons chopped cilantro

3 cups baby spinach leaves

Heat 1⅔ cups of the oil to 350°F in a pan large enough to allow for a decent gap between the surface of the oil and the top of the pan (to prevent the hot oil from bubbling over). Drop in the eggplant cubes and fry in small, manageable batches until golden brown. Carefully remove the eggplants from the oil using a slotted spoon and drain on paper towels. Set aside.

Heat the remaining oil in a large pot (if you're being thrifty, you can take this oil from the eggplant frying pan). Add the onion and garlic and cook until golden. Add all of the spices and give everything a good stir. Pour in the tomatoes, stir again, and bring to a simmer. Cook until around 90 percent of the liquid has bubbled away, stirring every now and then to prevent the mixture from catching.

Add the golden raisins and the salt, stir in the eggplant, and leave to cook for 5 minutes.

If you are making this in advance, leave to cool, then chill in the fridge until required. Just before serving, stir in the chopped herbs and baby spinach.

A WORD OF WARNING

If you leave the heat on under the oil while you cook the eggplant, it will keep getting hotter and hotter, which could lead to an explosion and your house burning down—and, in a worst-case scenario, this could delay dinner.

A fabulous curry featuring green leafy vegetables (sag) and potatoes (aloo).

There are hundreds of variations on this recipe, but I find the one below works consistently well. It can be served on the side of a meat curry, or try stirring in peas, paneer cheese, and cooked eggplant for a healthy vegetable curry in its own right. Every chef who has ever worked for me will know this recipe by heart!

Sag aloo

SERVES 4

1 tablespoon vegetable oil

2 onions, finely chopped

3 garlic cloves, chopped

1 cup fresh peeled and grated ginger

1 teaspoon black mustard seeds

1 teaspoon yellow mustard seeds

¾ teaspoon cumin seeds

½ teaspoon ground turmeric

½ teaspoon chile powder

1 teaspoon ground ginger

1 teaspoon salt

2 lbs potatoes, peeled and cut into bite-sized chunks

4 cups baby spinach leaves

Heat the oil and lightly fry the onion, garlic and ginger until golden brown—this could take 10 minutes or so. Add the spices and salt and cook for a minute, then tip in the potatoes and mix well. Pour over enough water to *almost half-cover* the potatoes—less is better than too much! Bring the water to a simmer, cover the pan, and cook until the potatoes are just cooked through.

Remove the pan from the heat and leave the potatoes to cool and absorb more of the excess liquid, which is a good thing. (You could skip this cooling maneuver and just stir in the spinach and serve, but I think it's important that the potatoes have time to absorb the cooking liquid so that they are flavored throughout.)

The finished dish needs to be moist but not too wet, so a little of the cooking liquid may need to be removed prior to reheating. When you are ready to serve, gently reheat the potatoes and stir in the spinach.

Onion bhajis

MAKES 6–8

2 cups very, very finely sliced onions

pinch of salt

1 teaspoon ground cumin

1 teaspoon ground coriander

1 teaspoon chile powder

½ teaspoon ground turmeric

2 cardamom pods, seeds only, ground to a powder

½ teaspoon garam masala

1 tablespoon chopped cilantro

5 mint leaves, finely shredded

1 teaspoon rice flour

¾ cup chickpea flour (also known as gram flour or besan—we may not need this much, but have it ready)

vegetable oil, for frying

Put the onions in a large bowl and sprinkle on the salt. Rub the salted onions by hand until they release a little moisture, then add the spices and rub these in too. Add the cilantro and mint leaves and mix. Add the rice flour and half of the chickpea flour and mix in really well by hand, adding a little of the remaining chickpea flour at a time (you may not need all of it), until the mixture forms a sticky batter. If the onions don't release much moisture, you may need to add a splash of water. I expect you will need to use at least 75 percent of the chickpea flour, but obviously some onions are juicier than others! You are looking for a batterlike consistency that combines the onions.

Pour the oil into a large pan to a depth of at least 4 inches and heat to 350°F. To test the mixture, roll a little into a ball and drop into the oil. Fry until golden brown, drain, and eat. If you think it's a little dry or if it breaks up in the oil, add more water to the mixture. If it is too wet to handle, add a little more chickpea flour. Once you are happy with the consistency, roll the mixture into 6–8 bhajis and fry until golden brown. Carefully remove from the oil using a slotted spoon, drain on paper towels, and serve.

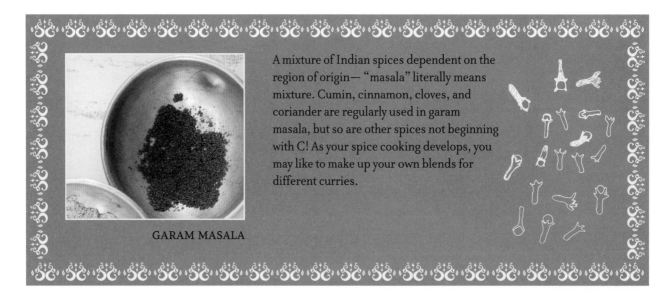

GARAM MASALA

A mixture of Indian spices dependent on the region of origin— "masala" literally means mixture. Cumin, cinnamon, cloves, and coriander are regularly used in garam masala, but so are other spices not beginning with C! As your spice cooking develops, you may like to make up your own blends for different curries.

66 I have a theory of evolution when it comes to cooking rice. Many, many years ago, someone, somewhere, recorded the very first rice-cooking recipe which suggested using ¼–⅓ cup raw rice per person. I don't know who that was, but I do know that they were either on a diet or that they wrote their recipe immediately after a big lunch because, frankly, they grossly underestimated the amount of rice the average person eats. The second person to include a rice-cooking recipe simply didn't bother with research and just copied down the same amount and this kept happening all the way down the line until this very book. Check your package of rice in the pantry—I bet it recommends cooking ⅓ cup per person. But that's just not enough—not in my house, anyway!

Basmati rice is often thought to be the tricky variety to cook because it's best cooked through absorption of steam rather than in excess boiling water. This means that getting the water level right is crucial. A Bangladeshi kitchen porter at The Ritz London taught me this method and though it may appear quirky, it guarantees perfect rice every time. The banana leaf mentioned in the title is just a neat little trick to keep steaming rice hot. It's not essential but is a nice touch. 99

Basmati rice in a banana leaf

DEFINITELY ENOUGH FOR 4

1 tablespoon vegetable oil

1 onion, finely chopped

1 garlic clove, finely chopped

1 star anise

small piece of cinnamon stick

5 cardamom pods

1⅔ cups Basmati rice

A NOTE ON COOKING RICE

Rice contains starch, and if you rub the grains together you will release that starch. In a risotto this is exactly what is needed, so you stir to release the starch and create a creamy texture. When cooking Basmati rice, you want to avoid releasing the starch or you will end up with a gummy, glue-like mess that will disappoint even your best friend. Always work the rice gently and carefully to avoid breaking or scratching the grains. Lecture over.

Heat the oil in a lidded pan large enough to allow the rice to swell by five or six times its volume as it cooks. Add the onion, garlic, star anise, cinnamon, and cardamom pods and cook for 3 minutes until the onion is softened but not colored.

Meanwhile, pour the rice into a sieve and rinse under cold running water for a minute. Allow the rice to drain, then add to the pan. Carefully stir using a wooden spoon.

Fill a large pitcher with cold water (I haven't given a measurement on purpose). Gently pour water into the pan until it just covers the rice. Put your index finger into the pan so the tip of your finger touches the rice, then pour in more water until it reaches the first joint of your finger (this may seem crazy, but it works). Now remove your finger!

Bring to a boil, cover the pan with foil and the lid to trap the steam, and cook for exactly 5 minutes, then switch off the heat and leave well alone for 20 minutes. Don't be tempted to lift the lid or the steam will escape.

Lift the lid and marvel at this ingenious idea. Lightly fluff up the cooked rice with a fork and serve

THE BANANA LEAF PART

This isn't an ingredient, more a piece of homemade kitchen equipment that adds a nice finish to your spicy efforts. Cut a disk of banana leaf twice the size of the bowl in which you will serve your rice. Make a cut from the center of the banana leaf to the edge and fold into a cone. Secure the cone with a toothpick and place on top of the rice, thus trapping the escaping steam and keeping the rice nice and hot.

66 Matar paneer must be one of the most-ordered side dishes in any Indian restaurant, and each establishment seems to have a slightly different take on this simple North Indian curry of peas and cheese. I've included a recipe for making your own paneer because it's so straightforward that it's well worth trying. However, some supermarkets stock paneer, so feel free to skip that part if you want an easier life. While this dish is often listed in the side-order section of a menu, there's no reason why it can't be a meal in itself—it really is that good. 99

Matar paneer (cheesy peas!)

SERVES 4

vegetable oil, for frying

1 large onion, finely chopped

3 garlic cloves, finely chopped

1 cup fresh peeled and grated ginger

1 teaspoon coriander seeds

1 teaspoon cumin seeds

1 teaspoon yellow mustard seeds

½ teaspoon red pepper flakes

1 teaspoon ground turmeric

10 curry leaves

14oz can chopped tomatoes

¾ cup coconut milk

1½ cups peas

FOR THE PANEER CHEESE

2 quarts whole milk

4 tablespoons lemon juice

If making your own paneer cheese, heat the milk in a pan large enough to allow the milk to bubble up as it boils. Bring the milk to a simmer, then add the lemon juice and start stirring. The milk will curdle as the curds and whey separate. Continue stirring until the curd coagulates into small lumps. Remove from the heat.

Line a large sieve or colander with a square of cheesecloth and place it over a bowl. Strain the milk through the cheesecloth and discard the whey.

Lift the cheese, still in the cheesecloth, out of the sieve and give it a gentle squeeze to remove any residual moisture. Wrap the cheese tightly in the cheesecloth, place into a dish, and place a heavy weight on top. We use a brick wrapped in foil.

Leave the weight in place for 40 minutes or until the cheese has condensed into a block. Either remove the cheese from the cheesecloth and use right away or leave it wrapped in the cheesecloth and chill in the fridge overnight.

And now for the cheesy peas. Heat a splash of oil in a pan over medium heat and toss in the onion, garlic, and ginger. Cook for a few minutes or until golden brown and softened, stirring every so often.

Meanwhile, grind the coriander seeds, cumin seeds, mustard seeds, and red pepper flakes to a powder in a mortar and pestle, then add to the pan along with the turmeric and curry leaves and stir well.

Add the tomatoes and cook until the juice has reduced by about half.

Pour in the coconut milk and bring to a simmer, then cook until a thick sauce forms—about 10 minutes.

At this point I tend to try a spot of multitasking. Break up 1½ cups of the paneer cheese, heat 1 tablespoon oil in a frying pan, and cook the paneer until lightly golden brown. Meanwhile, add the peas to the curry sauce and allow to simmer. Add the cheese to the peas and serve.

Lime cordial

MAKES 1 QUART OF SIMPLE SYRUP / RECIPE SERVES 4

FOR THE SIMPLE SYRUP

1 quart water

2 cups sugar

4 cardamom pods

7oz fresh ginger, unpeeled

8 lemongrass stalks

TO SERVE

ice

juice of 3–4 limes

20 mint leaves

still or sparkling water

To make the simple syrup, pour the water and sugar into a pan and bring to a simmer, stirring occasionally. Bash the cardamom pods, ginger, and lemongrass in a mortar and pestle and add to the pan. Continue to cook until reduced by half. Remove from the heat and leave to cool and infuse overnight.

Strain through a very fine sieve or cheesecloth and then decant into a sterilized bottle and store in the fridge for up to 2 weeks.

To serve, put a few ice cubes into four glasses and pour in the lime juice. Rub the mint leaves to bruise and add to the glasses. Fill each glass three-quarters full with still or sparkling water (I like fizzy water, but it's not a deal breaker).

Serve with a small pitcher of the simple syrup and let your guests add this to taste.

One of the keenest debates in the wine world centers around which wines (if any) go perfectly with spicy food. The Gewürztraminer grape produces an aromatic wine that many feel is the best match, while others prefer beer—Asian beers are very obviously the popular ones to serve with a curry or a bowl of hot Thai noodles. But there are other options, and I've included a couple in this chapter. Both make a darn good drink whether you are eating or not. This cordial works perfectly as a long, cool, nonalcoholic drink, but just to reassure my mother, it also works well with a double vodka shot added to it. Best of all, it's practically free!

Ironically (though I don't know whether they themselves have noted the irony), many of the finest and thus most expensive restaurants in the world have built their gastronomic reputations on (free) wild ingredients, foraged from their local area. Many of the restaurants that currently find themselves listed among the World's Best Restaurants go in for the noble pursuit of "wildculture," which basically amounts to foraging. If you are new to this trendy (yet centuries-old) gastronomic pursuit, I shall give you a very basic starting point so that you, too, can benefit from a bit of free food.

Elderflower is the blossom found growing on a tree called an elder. Obvious really, but you're a beginner, so I wanted to cover all bases. The blossom is a creamy, white color and is excellent for making cordial, from which you can create sorbets, granitas and jellies, or simply make into a great cold drink on a hot day. Later in the season, the blossom that you didn't pick will form clusters of dark berries—you guessed it, elderberries—which can be used to make jam or fruit pies.

I make industrial quantities of this cordial each season and freeze it in plastic bottles. This recipe is dedicated to the memory of my pal Stella, who was the elderflower queen of West London. Every year at the appropriate time I'd get a text telling me where I could find a bounty of blooms.

Elderflower & ginger cordial

MAKES ABOUT 2½ QUARTS

50 heads of elderflower
2½ quarts water
7¾ lbs sugar
3 lemons
10oz fresh ginger, unpeeled
5 tablespoons citric acid

Check the elderflowers to make sure there are no insects in residence, then set aside in a large bowl. You could even wash them if you want, but most foragers tend to skip this step.

Pour the water into a large pan, bring to a boil, and add the sugar.

Meanwhile, prepare the lemons. Peel 1 of the lemons and discard the peel, then halve all 3 and add them to the elderflowers. Bash the ginger to a pulp using a rolling pin, baseball bat, or similar implement of destruction, and throw it into the elderflower bowl. Pour the boiling water and sugar over the elderflowers, lemons, and ginger, and stir in the citric acid. Leave to stand at room temperature overnight.

Strain through a very fine sieve or cheesecloth and then decant into sterilized bottles. All you need now is a fabulous spicy recipe book (hang on… that's lucky) and some cold water to dilute the cordial. The cordial will keep in the freezer for up to 3 months, or in the fridge for up to 1 month.

Index

Acknowledgments

While one who is tasked with writing a book can, at times, feel lonely and isolated, there are, in truth, so many people who contributed in so many different ways...

Huge thanks to MJ, Ellie, and Richie for belief and support (and at times ruthless honesty!).

Big thanks, too, are due to my business partner Greg Bellamy and the whole team at The Victoria, especially my kitchen team, Charlie, Damo, Luke, Tom, Eloise, Tomas, Binay, and Will, for covering me when I was busy writing and for their help in developing, testing, retesting, and perfecting many of the recipes.

Thanks also to Nigel (the old man) and Coleen Merrett, Ali Guther, Anton Manganaro, Chris Marriott, Dan Pennington, Roger Elliot, Adam Gaunt-Evans, Melanie Jappy, and Bernard Zieja for spicy encouragement, inspiration, distraction and support—past and present.

Thanks to "Team DML," particularly Borra Garson and Jan Croxson, for pushing me into this in the first place.

And last but not least enormous thanks to the finest "book building" team ever—Kyle Cathie for giving me the chance, my (very patient and understanding) editor Sophie Allen, amazing photographer Jan Baldwin, Queen of props Lesley Dilcock, the world's most talented food stylist Annie Rigg, and designer and quirky doodler Anita Mangan.